THE
CAMPUS
BATTLEFIELD

HOW CONSERVATIVES CAN WIN THE
BATTLE ON CAMPUS AND WHY IT MATTERS

CHARLIE KIRK

A POST HILL PRESS BOOK

The Campus Battlefield:
How Conservatives Can WIN the Battle on Campus and Why It Matters
© 2018 by Charlie Kirk
All Rights Reserved

ISBN: 978-1-64293-094-8
ISBN (eBook): 978-1-64293-095-5

Cover art by Rebecca Wiley

Post Hill Press
New York • Nashville
posthillpress.com

Published in the United States of America

Contents

Foreword

I have always loved a good fight.

Since I was young my father taught me the importance of standing up for what you believe in. I learned the value of never backing down and never surrendering. It doesn't matter how long or how hard that fight might take—you do whatever it takes and you fight like hell, and you win. America is a land of winners; it is in this nation's DNA and runs through the blood of our patriots.

My father is fighting for America every single day. He is fighting against special interests in both political parties that have been happy to manage the decline of our great country. My father went down the escalator in June of 2015 to change all of that. He ran on a message of unity, American exceptionalism, the rule of law, and the value of hard work. He ran and is now governing with a mantra of Making America Great Again!

They said he would never run for President.

They said he couldn't win the primary.

They said he couldn't beat crooked Hillary.

They said he would be a failed President.

And he continues to prove the elites wrong! When my father spoke of how much wins there would be for our nation, he wasn't joking. He was serious.

After a short time in office we have seen the best economic numbers in American history, a booming stock market, exploding consumer confidence the largest tax cut ever, ISIS being destroyed, peace being brokered all throughout the world, and a return of American exceptionalism.

I have dedicated my time and energy to defending my father, his agenda, and our movement. His Presidency will largely dictate the course of the future of America and the future of the world.

But there is another war brewing in America that people need to engage in that is even bigger than politics: the culture war, happening on college campuses every single day.

I am stunned when I turn on my TV to see twenty-year-old students demanding safe spaces, protesting America, burning our flag, calling my father a Nazi, and then, are offended if anyone dares to question their viewpoint. The left wing Marxist influence upon our youth has grown totally and completely out of control and is infecting the soul of our great country.

During the summer of 2016 I met Charlie Kirk. He was twenty-two years old at the time, and I will admit, I had my reservations. We already had enough political novices working on our campaign, and the last thing I wanted was another young kid who had no idea what he was doing.

But the more time I spent with Charlie Kirk and the more I learned about Turning Point USA, the more I realized there was something unique that we were missing.

Our core team soon adopted Charlie to travel the country with us to plan events, hit college campuses, and barnstorm the country. It was a rag tag army of Gentry Beach, Tommy Hicks, and Charlie Kirk. We were all volunteers, none of us paid by the campaign but together we raised over 150 million dollars in ninety days, spoke at over 213 events, did 195 media hits, and I took countless selfies.

Charlie had me speaking on college campuses drawing thousands of students from Michigan, Ohio, Iowa, Pennsylvania, Florida, and Wisconsin. We were drawing bigger crowds than Hillary on her home turf!

After we shocked the world and won the election I got more and more involved with Turning Point USA. I saw the sophistication of the organization, the depth of its leadership, the wisdom behind the outreach, the long-term vision embedded in their decisions, and the professionalism of their staff. I began to speak at more of their events, including keynoting the 2017 Student Action Summit in Palm Beach, FL to over three thousand students from all fifty states.

In this book Charlie Kirk has outlined the core issues infecting college campuses and how we can reclaim them from the left. No fight can be more important than this one for the future of our country and the next generation.

Charlie Kirk is a fighter. He fights hard and fights smart. He knows we are in a war for the soul of America and has a battle plan to win. Charlie understands what is at stake. He understands that we must fight for America on high school and college campuses. Our movement needs Charlie Kirk and Turning Point USA.

Please enjoy this book, share it with your friends, support Turning Point USA, and get involved. The fight is only beginning, and we need your help to save the greatest country ever to exist. We cannot do this alone.

For Making America Great Again,
Donald J. Trump Jr.

Introduction

Who could have imagined that I would need police protection to talk about freedom on a university campus? A university, of all places, whose very essence is the freedom to pursue knowledge and wisdom, no matter where it takes us.

Yet here I was, needing eight private security agents and thirty police officers to secure my safety at the University of Illinois at Urbana-Champaign so I could deliver another of my "Smashing Socialism" lectures.

As I climbed onto the stage, the wild screaming got louder and louder: "Charlie Kirk is a jerk! Charlie Kirk is a jerk!" Nice alliteration, that, but I've been called worse. Like the other chant rising up from the crowd, "Hey hey, ho ho, this Nazi has got to go."

"Go," as in, "go away. Don't come here. You have no right to be here." Of course, the University of Illinois and I are not alone. Suppression of free speech by the authoritarian left has become a dangerous movement on college campuses across America. Scheduled speakers are abused and threatened. Open classroom discussion is stifled. Conservative students are intimidated.

But I wasn't going to cave in. Cancelling the event and letting down the students who came to hear me with open or supportive minds was not an option. In the audience were leaders and members of the Turning Point USA chapter of the University of Illinois. But there were more; the hall was filled with hundreds of other students who wanted to listen and learn. Despite the threats that we had received since announcing the event, we were determined that it would go on as planned.

It was worth it. I was greeted by a standing ovation. Overwhelming, in fact. It took my breath away, seeing some students going absolutely wild in support as I took the podium. For the next forty minutes, I laid out the core ideas of what Turning Point USA believes, the culture battle we are fighting, and the pro-freedom solutions we are advocating.

Opening it up for questions was even more gratifying. Most student engagement with me was friendly. After five or six questions, I noticed a common theme: Most had come there to genuinely learn another point of view. They were curious about what conservatives believed. Thank God, their leftist professors had not snuffed out their intellectual inquisitiveness, an increasingly common practice these days on American college campuses. After fielding about twenty questions in the same vein, we left through the basement to avoid the intellectually challenged, brassy protestors whose minds were closed to anything that they weren't instructed to believe.

Driving back to Chicago, I reflected on the event and was struck again by how intellectually curious the University of Illinois students were. They really wanted to learn and see another point of view. There was something good happening on American campuses that the media was ignoring. It was a spark that could grow into a bonfire.

This experience kept playing itself out as I visited more and more schools across the country: Cleveland State University, University of Minnesota, Florida International University, and Eastern Carolina University. At each, I was met with resistance from far-left radicals, but I saw first-hand thousands and thousands of students curious to learn more about America, free enterprise, and the Constitution.

> *If conservative ideas were truly that bad & unpopular why does the left try to censor them? Why do activists shout down speakers? If no one liked our ideas, no one would follow us, attend our speeches, or engage with us. It is because the left is scared we might be winning.*
>
> —*@charliekirk11*

While I witnessed how our colleges were doing a serious disservice to students by trying to teach them out of an intellectually bankrupt leftist playbook, I saw something else, something hopeful. Here, indeed, was evidence before my eyes that despite the best efforts of an ideologically rigid faculty to indoctrinate students, many do indeed want to hear a conservative approach to economics and politics.

Sadly, the powers that run colleges today—the faculty, administration, and some alumni who have mindlessly bought the prevailing authoritarian and leftist agenda—no longer believe a college is a place where different ideas are taught, expressed and challenged. They have become leftist echo chambers that reinforce an anti-American, anti-freedom, pro-Marxist worldview.

The institutional dominance the left enjoys did not happen overnight. The left doggedly planned for decades to take over our high schools and our colleges. The left relentlessly and incrementally pounded its credos into the minds of generations of students. And today we are seeing the disastrous results.

Throughout this book, I will examine how the left has pulled this off and how we can resurrect the heart and soul of our universities as—yes—safe places for the teaching and expression of *all* ideas, not just those endorsed by the liberal curia. We have already begun this rescue mission, as Turning Point USA has a presence on more than one thousand American campuses. As the founder and executive director of Turning Point USA, I have become knowledgeable about leftist indoctrination in colleges. As such, I am able to deeply dive into how the left is strangling the meaning of a university and the tactics they have used to monopolize the academy. But we're not leaving it at that. Here you will read of our counter-offensive, how we are exposing doctrinaire professors for what they are, how we are standing tall for freedom in the face of reprehensible hostility, and how we are organizing a nation-wide movement that will, for the first time, challenge the left in their own house.

But this fight is over more than control of high schools and colleges. This is a life-or-death fight for the future of our country and of Western Civilization. If the leftist corruption of the ideas of liberty, free speech, and economic freedom now so common on college campuses comes to dominate the nation's outlook, as the left intends, this will not be a country that the Founding Fathers would recognize. It will be unrecognizable to all of us, who as Americans grew up enjoying the very freedoms that they now are trying to destroy.

We are at war for the soul of our country, and it's a fight we must win before it is too late.

1

Your Job Is to Shut Up and Listen

"How can you say that America is a good place?"

The student was incredulous that I could make such a bold and, to her, dishonest assertion. The very idea violated everything she had learned from her college professors, and now she was challenging me in one of my frequent college lectures that I give about liberty, the free market, and conservative values.

She wasn't ranting. She wasn't being nasty. It was just that it was so outside her experience that she couldn't believe that anyone would actually defend America. And it was a great question. It went to the heart of what Turning Point USA is all about, and it deserved an answer.

It's a question often posed by middle-class college students. These mostly are young men and women who enjoy the very fruits of liberty and the free market that allows them to go to college, get a degree, and pursue a career of their choosing. Less than 7 percent of the world's population has what 40 percent of Americans have: a college degree.

If America is so bad, why do so many people want in? Millions are so anxious to come to America that they're literally climbing over fences, swimming rivers, and figuratively busting down doors. Those are just the illegal immigrants. Add to that the millions who come to America legally, waiting patiently for their immigration paperwork to clear.

If America is so bad, why is it the most generous country in the world, the first to show up with food, water, and other life-saving aid for those whose lives have been devastated by natural disasters? If America is so bad, why do we give away billions in foreign aid to struggling countries? Why are we the biggest supporters of the United Nations, despite its hostility to our values? If America is so bad, why does it lead the world in creativity, inventiveness, and discovery, supplying the world with the building blocks of progress? If America is so bad, why has it survived for more than two centuries as the world's most successful democracy and its values emulated by freedom-loving people around the world?

This kind of blindness to America's goodness is being taught and learned in colleges and universities across the land. Even in some high schools. It is symptomatic of The Closing of the Academic Mind.

It has made discourse—the heart of the idea of a university—nearly impossible and has eaten away at respect for conflicting views. This isn't just a problem for higher education; it is a threat to self-government. Self-government is based on the premise that answers are not handed down from an elite, all-knowing hierarchy. It is powered by debate that can lead to a consensus about the direction of our future path.

This is no easy task. Our Founding Fathers well knew this as they struggled to find a better way to govern than, on one hand, the monarchies, dictatorships, and oligarchies of Europe. Or, on the other hand, the anarchy of the bloody Reign of Terror that gripped France after its experiment with democracy failed so miserably. Finding balance between authoritarianism and anarchy is difficult, indeed.

So, how is this idea not in danger when America's future leaders are being taught that emotional and physical comfort is valued above rigorous debate, that avoiding offense is more important than protecting freedom of expression, that free speech can be silenced because it might hurt someone's feelings?

> *College social justice training 101: Whoever gets declared to be the biggest victim then is allowed to become the biggest bully.*
>
> —*@charliekirk11, May 9, 2018*

Let's look at a disturbing example of how this has played out:

It started when an ethics teacher at a Catholic university banned classroom discussion about same-sex marriage because it would be "homophobic." How incredible is that? Traditional marriage is a precept of the Catholic Church, reaffirmed by its leader, Pope Francis. If by wild chance the pope had dropped in on the class, would the teacher still have banned its discussion?

It happened at Marquette University, a Jesuit school in Milwaukee, where a graduate teaching assistant told the class that they would skip over any discussion of same-sex marriage because it was a subject that everyone agreed on, adding that if anyone didn't concede that same-sex marriage should be legal, they should see her after class.

An undergraduate student took her up on it and brought along an audio recorder. Here's how their conversation went, transcribed from the recording, when he asked why he couldn't, in a course taught at a Catholic university, discuss something that the church itself teaches:

Teacher: Ok, there are some opinions that are not appropriate that are harmful, such as racist opinions, sexist opinions, and quite honestly, do you know if anyone in the class is homosexual?

Student: No, I don't.

Teacher: And don't you think that that would be offensive to them if you were to raise your hand and challenge this?

Student: If I choose to challenge this, it's my right as an American citizen.

Teacher: Ok, well, actually you don't have a right in this class, as—especially as an ethics professor to make homophobic comments, racist comments, sexist comments....

Student: Homophobic comments? They're not. I'm not saying that gays, that one guy can't like another girl or something like that. Or, one guy can't like another guy.

Teacher: This is about restricting rights and liberties of individuals. Um and just as I would take offense if women can't serve in XYZ positions because that is a sexist comment.

Student: I don't have any problem with women saying that. I don't have any problem with women joining anything like that.

Teacher: No, I'm saying that if you are going to make a comment like that, it would be similar to making a....

Student: Absolutely.

Teacher: How I would experience would be similar to how someone who is in this room and who is homosexual who would experience someone criticizing this.

Student: Ok, so because they are homosexual I can't have my opinions? And it's not being offensive towards them because I am just having my opinions on a very broad subject.

Teacher: You can have whatever opinions you want but I can tell you right now, in this class homophobic comments, racist comments, and sexist comments will not be tolerated. If you don't like that you are more than free to drop this class.

Student: So, are you saying that not agreeing with gay marriage is homophobic?

Teacher: To argue about that individuals should not have rights is going to be offensive to someone in this class.

How odd to punish someone for expressing views that align with Catholic teaching about marriage and family. For asserting in a Catholic classroom that defending traditional marriage is "homophobic," comparable to racism and sexism. For a teacher to incorrectly assert that a student has no right as a citizen to challenge something said in the classroom. Or that being an "ethics professor" gives her special authority to silence a student. Or that he should vamoose if he disagrees. That the mere possibility that someone *might* be offended is enough to avoid discussing a controversial subject. Never mind if you know for certain that someone is there who will be offended.

> *"The further a society drifts from the truth, the more it will hate those who speak it."*
> —@charliekirk11, quoting George Orwell

But this is only half the story. When the student tried to register his complaint with the academic authorities, he basically got nowhere. He was ignored. He was even threatened for recording the conversation. He ended up dropping the class. If he felt offended, his feelings didn't seem to count. The feelings of people with traditional or conservative views simply don't count.

There's more. A conservative faculty member (how rare is that?) came to the student's defense on his blog. For which John McAdams, a tenured political science professor, found himself in a heap of trouble. He was excoriated by the administration, investigated, suspended without pay, condemned by a star chamber of other faculty members, barred from being on Marquette's campus, and, finally, fired.

So, instead of disciplining the teacher for violating the student's rights and academic freedom, the university conducted a nasty, career-ending campaign against the professor who defended free expression. In violation, one might add, of the university's own policy and contract with McAdams that are supposed to ensure his free speech.

In a tacit admission that a university can't discipline, silence, or fire someone for expressing his views, the administration came up with a dubious claim that McAdams was guilty of speech that endangered the teacher. The evidence? She received 135 emails or letters, of which forty-nine supported her. Only eighteen of the ones that criticized her were truly harassing, according to court documents in a suit McAdams filed challenging his dismissal. That was the sum and substance of what Marquette University President Michael R. Lovell described as "a *flood* of violent threats and hateful messages." (Emphasis added.)

In a letter-to-the-editor responding to a *Wall Street Journal* editorial criticizing the university for its authoritarian behavior, Lovell wrote: "John McAdams has the right to talk about controversial topics on his blog and to disagree with and debate Marquette-related positions freely. But he crossed the line when he launched a personal, demeaning Internet attack on a Marquette student, choosing to publicly shame her to advance his narrative and draw attention to himself and his blog."

This "student" was actually the teacher who banned discussion of gay marriage in her classroom. To call her simply a "student" is disingenuous. She was in what the left likes to call a superior, more powerful position—someone who can intimidate and punish someone lower on the ladder. This is the teacher who conducted her own nasty campaign against McAdams, calling him a "bigoted moron," an "uncritical, creepy homophobic person with bad argumentation skills," "a flaming bigot, sexist and homophobic idiot." Oh, he also was guilty of having an "ugly face." Also, according to the lawsuit, the teacher's boss, the Marquette philosophy department's chair, referred to McAdams in writing as a "right wing lunatic." The chair also called the conservative student who had complained about the teacher an "insulin [sic] little twerp," a "little twit," and a "jackass." How is that for the left employing the personal attack tactics that they routinely accuse the right of using?

This is the teacher who earlier had tried and failed to transfer to a university with a more prestigious philosophy department and who then used the publicity from the episode to be accepted by the school and secure financial aid. Meanwhile, a Milwaukee County judge, in a supremely ironic ruling, sided with Marquette and dismissed McAdams' suit, saying, "academic freedom does not mean that a faculty member can harass, threaten, intimidate, ridicule, or impose his or her views on students." Ironic, because that's exactly what the teacher did by banning discussion of same-sex marriage in her classroom. As of this writing, the Wisconsin Supreme Court has agreed to hear the case on direct appeal.

As a private institution, Marquette is not bound by the same First Amendment guarantees as a public university. But that doesn't mean that Marquette is free and clear of guilt for stomping on the student's and McAdams' rights. Or for betraying the idea of a university that has held sway for centuries.

So, here in a nutshell is but one example of the authoritarian culture that the left has created in the academe. Here is how one student was told to shut up and listen. Here is how the faculty and administration formed a Greek Chorus of mindless reciters of the given left-wing dogma. Here is how they punish anyone who steps out of line, by defaming and depriving the defender of liberty of his livelihood. Here is how subject matter that is, of itself contentious, settled ex cathedra. Here is how America's future leaders are being corrupted.

And there's more.

2

"I Don't Think It Is 'Safe' to Be Conservative On Our Campus"

How ironic that all those lectures about the desperate need for campus safe spaces and trigger warnings and the wickedness of microaggressions and offensive speech come from the left. It's ironic because liberals are most often the aggressors. Conservatives are shamed, shunned, excluded, and exiled. Micro- and macro-aggressions against conservatives are tolerated, if not applauded.

But it's not conservatives who are calling for safe spaces and the rest to protect themselves from having their feelings hurt. In comparison to liberals, how often do conservatives organize boisterous demonstrations to prevent liberal speakers from appearing on campus? How often do conservatives harass liberals as they try to recruit students to their causes? How often do conservatives say that liberal free speech must be restricted because it is hateful and offensive? How often do conservatives march on administrative offices to force the cancellation of liberal speakers? How many conservatives are demanding "safe spaces" that are essentially echo chambers for liberal bombast? How often? Not often, if ever.

Self-styled "progressives" are the ones who are snuffing out free speech and making the expression of conservative ideas a risky venture, betraying the culture of free speech that liberals not too long ago praised and aggressively defended. When it comes to hostile campus environments, it's difficult to find any surpassing the ones progressives, liberals, and far-left clans are creating for conservatives.

> *At Miami college founded by Cubans exiled under communism, officials shut down pro-capitalism club.*
> —@charliekirk11, April 10, 2017

Again and again, I hear from our more than one thousand Turning Point USA campus chapters about left-wing efforts to shut them up and shut them down. So, too, do I hear from our regional field reps of instances of liberals hurling offensive language and threatening actions against our members.

One that got national attention was on the University of Nebraska-Lincoln (UNL) campus, where sophomore Kaitlyn Mullen had set up a table in front of the Nebraska Union on the first Friday of the Fall 2017 semester to recruit students for Turning Point. She was wearing one of our popular "Big Government Sucks" T-shirts and the table was arrayed with our literature and posters.

Our Midwest field rep takes up the story:

I got a call from Kaitlyn, telling me that she was having trouble. She said that a faculty member was there now and telling her she was not in the free speech zone. The teacher told Kaitlyn that she had to take her table and leave.

I told her, "Under no circumstances are you to leave." But when Kaitlyn stayed the faculty member carried through on her threat to call the police to have her evicted. An officer arrived, checked out the situation and said he didn't see an issue there. He understood the law, that it's a public university, where free speech is protected under the First Amendment. He left without telling Kaitlyn she had to go.

Then a couple of other faculty members showed up, berating and intimidating her. As I'm listening on the phone, they accuse her of advocating white nationalism and having KKK leanings. I told her to record it. They were circling her table. One is giving Kaitlyn the finger. They scream the f-word at her. Kaitlyn was no threat; she didn't deserve that. We advocate for lower taxes. Smaller government. Capitalism. For this she was called a neo-fascist. We didn't know that reducing the size of federal government all of a sudden is fascism.

Here I'll break in to say that apparently, these college professors are so ignorant of history—not surprising these days—that they don't know that fascism is defined as a centralized, autocratic government that imposes severe economic and social regimentation and forcible suppression of opposition. Exactly everything that Turning Point is fighting against. Back to story:

> Kaitlyn ended up in tears as a result. The cops showed up again. A bystander had called them, concerned about her, wondering if she was okay. They escorted her home in tears.
>
> The university later reached out to her. Oh, they were so sorry about what had happened. They wanted to meet with her. I know how intimidation works, so I flew in to be with her for her meeting with them. They said the usual stuff, how they'd launch an investigation.

What other choice did they have? Nebraska Governor Pete Ricketts and a few influential legislators were on the school's case, noting that all the national publicity was giving the state a black eye and wrecking the university's reputation. They had to do something.

One thing they did was to circle the wagons. Emails obtained through a Freedom of Information Act request revealed that the public relations staff wanted to aggressively blow back. One email, "Have a surrogate(s) submit op-eds" to the *Omaha World-Herald* and *Lincoln Journal Star* as "aggressive counter-measures" to coverage of the matter. Another email mentioned how Turning Point was clubbing the university with the incident every day.

But this was not the face that university President Hank Bounds wanted to show to the world. After the emails were made public, Bounds wrote an open letter to Governor Ricketts that the emails surprised and embarrassed him. "Some of the emails reflect unprofessional behavior by our employees and I apologize," Bounds said.

One of the emails, however, tended to indict the university for creating a hostile environment for conservatives. Ellen Weissinger, the emeritus senior vice chancellor of academic affairs, had noted the hostility that conservatives regularly face on campus: "But the real issue is that we've got to do more to advance civility on campus. And frankly campuses have to become more tolerant and welcoming to conservative students and faculty. This has worried me for years. I don't think it is 'safe' to be conservative on our campus. Too many faculty espouse their personal political views as gospel in classes were there [*sic*] views have no relevance."

Probably in the face of criticism, Weissinger later wrote a clarification, saying that she had actually been trying in the first email to support the steps the university was taking to ensure everyone's voice is heard. She said she should have "expressed my strongly held personal opinions more thoughtfully that day." It's worth quoting her letter at length.

> To be honest, that day I was recalling the feeling of advocacy and protectiveness I felt about students and faculty during my administration career. It has always been the chief academic officer's job to "worry" about whether every member of the campus community can speak their mind. During my administrative career, I did worry that conservative students might feel less welcomed about expressing their view points. I worried about international students and first-generation students, too. Maybe most of all I worried about

students involved in the Black Lives Matter movement. I always felt that it was my job to do what I could to assure that our campus was a place where all viewpoints were drawn into the conversation and considered. In a meritocracy of ideas, everyone needs a chance to talk and every idea needs a fair chance to win the day. As the world around us becomes more polarized, universities need to work even harder to foster open and civil discourse. That principle is a centerpiece of my personal vision for all campuses.

Don't get me wrong—in the thirty-one years I was a faculty member at UNL, I never once worried that any student was physically unsafe because of their political or social or intellectual perspectives. "Safety" in an academic community is about feeling invited to express your argument. Really effective faculty members create classrooms and labs and studios in which that invitation is at the forefront. There are a small number of faculty members on any campus who don't share that vision of college teaching. Even one is too many for me.

My thanks to Weissinger for her candor. We applaud her statement that we deserve (almost) as much protection of our viewpoint as does Black Lives Matter. We completely agree that "safety" is defined as "feeling invited to express your argument." And with the need for teachers to create an atmosphere "in which that invitation is at the forefront." Unlike the hideous way, as described in the previous chapter, in which Marquette University punished a conservative professor who also felt that way. As for there being only a "small number of faculty members who don't share that vision," we don't agree, as we'll show later.

In case anyone missed it in Weissinger's letter, President Bounds underscored that her reference to "safety" was not about actual physical assault. He emphasized that he and Chancellor Ronnie Green "have met with hundreds of students, of many backgrounds and beliefs, and not one identifying as conservative has told us they felt threatened. UNL has a reporting line that allows any member of the campus community to report incidents, anonymously if they wish. No student identifying as conservative has filed a report."

Again, the point is about conservative students being intimidated, harassed and threatened. We are not asserting that conservative students are suffering wholesale physical attacks. Implying that this is only about physical attacks is simply a diversion.

Then, to emphasize that the school was not deaf to our concerns, Bounds wrote, "Nonetheless, I know there are concerns about bias on our campuses," and he proceeded to outline steps he has taken to ensure open and safe discussion. Among them are developing "a plan to ensure that no inappropriate political bias exists in our classrooms or anywhere else on campus"; soliciting advice from all "stakeholders" about "matters related to free speech"; engaging Gallup to conduct "an assessment of the campus environment for students, faculty and staff of diverse political backgrounds"; and directing Chancellor Green to write a letter to all students "to remind them of our commitment to free speech and provide them with specific options for recourse if they feel they have been treated unfairly."

Well and good. Not that we haven't heard this before from schools all over the country. The proof will be in the pudding and we hope that these steps provide protection for conservatives and everyone else.

But for President Bounds' benefit, here's how one conservative student felt threatened. Writing for Fresh U, a site featuring freshmen writing about freshmen, Samantha Losurdo described "What It's Really Like Being A Conservative on a Liberal Campus."

She said, "As an 18-year-old college student who is a Conservative Republican, I do not feel respected by most at my school, nor do I feel safe." She explained how conservative Republicans must hold back their thoughts while hearing classmates "word vomit" the values that "our kind have." If she declared to anyone she is a conservative Republican, she was "sure that I would be labeled as a racist, women-hating, homophobic, Islamophobic bigot."

Even in the classroom, the very heart of intellectual inquiry, Losurdo said, "nine out of ten students who are Liberal Democrats are ready to bite off of [sic] your head and spit it on the ground when something doesn't sound right to them. People are ridiculously quick to shut you down without even hearing your explanation of thinking." She told of a student whose teacher warned her class that she would downgrade them if they had different political views.

Samantha Losurdo genuinely feared retaliation for her views. For too many conservative students, that fear remains unspoken. In that regard, their "safety" indeed feels threatened. As our field rep put it, "The biggest thing that conservative students fear isn't losing friends and not being invited to social outings. Although that does matter. But the biggest thing is grades. They worry that their grades will suffer and about everything else that comes with a bad mark. Do I speak up with my viewpoint? If I speak up in class to disagree with the teacher, will my grades suffer?"

While most intimidation on campus is of the psychological and emotional kinds, instances of a hostile environment that's physical or illegal are not unknown. Again, if Bounds needs evidence, here are a couple of examples.

First, Tariq Khan, a University of Illinois at Urbana-Champaign graduate instructor in history, reportedly violently went after some Turning Point USA students for daring to respond to his speech at a campus anti-Trump rally.

Joel Valdez, a freshman and campus activism coordinator for Turning Point USA, said he and some friends had gone to an anti-Trump rally on campus. Spotting them, Khan began shouting at the group, calling them white supremacists. Valdez replied, "Don't you have anything better to do with your time? Don't you have kids?" According to Valdez, Khan charged the group, accusing them of threatening his children, a completely unfounded and ludicrous exaggeration of Valdez's question.

"Khan immediately charged us, pushing us, throwing punches. We then attempted to defuse the situation and remained calm, but Tariq was uncontrollable and unhinged. I'm certain that Khan knew there was no threat; he just wanted to look for a fight. I wasn't interested," Valdez told the *Daily Illini*, the student newspaper. Eventually, Khan grabbed one of the group's cell phones, walked away with it and finally forcefully threw it on the ground, breaking it, Valdez said.

Police later charged Khan with a misdemeanor, criminal damage to property. As of this writing, the charges were pending. Khan has proclaimed his innocence, but the incident was recorded and went viral on the internet.

Here's a second example, and it also involves the University of Illinois at Urbana-Champaign. A professor of media and cinema studies, Jay Rosenstein, took his campaign against a popular and revered school mascot, Chief Illiniwek, into a public bathroom where he got himself arrested for video recording people inside.

Rosenstein has made a career of ridding the world of any memory of the Chief, who was retired in 2007 in the face of criticism of it being "offensive." It wasn't exactly that. Most students and alumni relished the sight of the respected Chief, who wore a feathered headdress and beaded buckskin, as he danced at athletic and other events. Not at all like the Cleveland Indians' degrading Chief Wahoo logo, Chief Illiniwek symbolized strength, courage and determination, qualities fans wanted to see in their athletic teams.

So the Chief never disappeared from campus, as his passionate fans, unofficially dressed in the Chief's regalia, regularly appeared at school events—an exercise of free speech and freedom of association. And so, when Rosenstein spied the Chief at an Illini (yes, the school and the state still are allowed to keep their honorifics of the Native Americans of Illinois) game, he tracked the "offender," whom he thought might be a school employee, to the washroom to, as he put it, catch the Chief putting on his costume to "document all of the ways the university employees might be involved in helping." Except that taking pictures of someone in a bathroom is illegal and a felony.

Rosenstein was arrested and led away in handcuffs, but get this: The local prosecutor, Julia Rietz, declined to press charges, explaining that she does so in cases involving cameras hidden in bathrooms "to record unknowing victims for the offenders' sexual gratification." But, she added, "While the arrest was technically appropriate, there was no evidence of such intent here." So, it appears that using a camera in a University of Illinois washroom just for the heck of it is legal.

Unlike Bounds, we don't need a study to know that liberal bias against conservatives is alive and well in classrooms and curricula, and among faculty, staff, administrators and even students. Let's explore some of the many examples.

3

The Magisterial Classroom Lectern

Are you a closet conservative?

When you walk into the first day of class, do you wonder if the teacher will ridicule you in front of the class if you express your conservative views? If the teacher's remarks betray him as a leftist, do you decide that you had better keep your mouth shut? Do you blanch at the prospect of an essay exam in which you might have to disagree with the teacher's political views? Do you sacrifice your beliefs for the sake of a better or a passing grade?

This is beyond unfair. It is dangerous.

It stifles the very idea of a university. It breeds dishonesty. It suppresses discourse.

It is divisive. It corrodes the outlook of a generation of future leaders who, living in the real world, need to learn that self-government works, not by the kind of autocratic declarations so prevalent in many classrooms today, but by mutual understanding, respect and the simple act of listening thoughtfully to each other—a disappearing virtue.

Once liberals were dedicated defenders of free speech. Today, campus "progressives" have turned that honorable heritage upside down by deputizing themselves to suppress free speech, deceiving themselves into believing that they are actually protecting free speech.

Under the guise of learning, instead comes opinion, judgment or pure propaganda. It's amazing what's passing for scholarship in college and even high school classrooms these days. What follows is a small sampling of magisterial leftist pronouncements itemized on Turning Point's Professor Watchlist (https://www.professorwatchlist.org), compiled from credible news sources:

> Professor Rochelle Gutierrez, University of Illinois, argued in a book that algebraic and geometry skills perpetuate "unearned privilege" among whites. "On many levels, mathematics itself operates as Whiteness. Who gets credit for doing and developing mathematics, who is capable in mathematics, and who is seen as part of the mathematical community is generally viewed as White," Gutierrez argued.

Melina Abdullah, chair of the California State University-Los Angeles Department of Pan-African Studies, wants investors to celebrate "Black Xmas" by divesting from "white corporations" and fighting "White Capitalism." She declared, "We know that state-sanctioned violence is rooted in White-supremacist capitalism."

Colleges have become Marxist indoctrination centers and left-wing activist training camps 10.4–1 ratio of Democrat to Republican professors at an average college 39% of top tier liberal arts have ZERO GOP professors.

　　　　　　　　　　　　　　　—@charliekirk11, May 11, 2017

Dr. Dana Cloud, a professor of communication and rhetorical studies at Syracuse University and a member of the International Socialist Organization, blames America for 9/11. Writing a new Pledge of Allegiance, she pledged allegiance to the people of Iraq, Palestine and Afghanistan, and "to their struggles to survive and resist slavery to corporate greed, brutal wars against their families, and the economic and environmental ruin wrought by global capitalism."

William Penn, a teacher in the Creative Writing Program at Michigan State University, was recorded complaining in one of his classes about "dead white Republicans" who "raped his country."

Angela Putman, assistant communications professor at Penn State-Brandywine and known as the "WhitePrivDoc," believes meritocracy is a "whiteness ideology." It's an example of how white people are "socialized to believe that [they] got where [they] are" because of individual effort. She beats herself up for her own whiteness, writing, "Learning to grapple with my own whiteness, white guilt, and my participation (whether explicit or implicit) in systems that are inherently racist is a constant struggle; but, it is one that I feel compelled and responsible to engage in, for as long as it takes to witness change—within me and within U.S. American society (ies)."

Dr. Todd Couch, a sociology professor at Coker College in South Carolina, said that "racial oppression" was central to the Founding Fathers' philosophy. According to a student in his class, Couch likes to lecture on white supremacy, the evilness of conservatives, and racial oppression. The student's notes declare that the Marxist perspective is "common among social sciences in all disciplines."

Dr. Chris Hamilton, a professor at Washburn University, accused conservatives, such as Ron Paul and Ted Cruz, of working to strip people of civil rights. He wrote in his class curriculum about "Neo-Confederacy movements that are part of Big Money ultra-right powers (Koch Industries, co-founders of the John Birch Society) that is part of the broad New White Nationalist movement." Hamilton's class was originally intended to cover the history of the 1960s civil rights movement.

Anthony Zenkus, a Columbia University School of Social Work lecturer, defended socialism by blaming capitalism for two world wars, centuries of slavery, and the genocide of Native Americans. He agreed with the mistaken assertion that the Reverend Martin Luther King "was a socialist before it was cool."

Alba Lamar, a graduate student and instructor at Michigan State University, taught students how to argue with conservatives about issues such as illegal immigration, refugees, and the Dakota Access pipeline when they go home for Thanksgiving. She mocked Christians for not supporting taking in Middle Eastern refugees and said conservatives often come to their views through fear.

Alvin Lee, a Human Resources Training Specialist at Purdue University, taught a class that such phrases as, "America is a melting pot," "Where are you from," "There is only one race, the human race," "Everyone can succeed in society if they work hard enough," and "I believe the most qualified person should get the job" are microaggressions and offensive statements. White people cannot be "color blind," he declared. Instead of attempting to encourage unity, he would rather encourage division and play diversity bingo to highlight our racial differences.

Dr. Andrew Kent Hallam, an English professor at Metropolitan State University of Denver, allegedly harassed and bullied Republican students. In his freshman composition class, he encouraged the majority of liberals in the class to repeatedly deride Republicans. Then he gave his new class its first assignment; an essay criticizing Alaska Governor Sarah Palin. In the piece, the students were to contradict the "fairy tale image of Palin" presented at the recent Republican National Convention. She was to be compared to Sleeping Beauty, according to written instructions.

Brent Terry, a part-time adjunct at Eastern Connecticut State University, was recorded in a class stating that if Republicans won in the 2014 election, colleges would close. He asserted that "racist, misogynist, money-grubbing people" are suppressing liberal votes.

Alicia Chavez, a lecturer at the University of Southern California, banned students from using the phrase "illegal immigrant" on their final exam.

Dr. Adam Kotsko, an Assistant Professor of Humanities at Shimer College, took to Twitter to justify the Charlie Hebdo shootings over what he called "hate speech." When Kotsko received backlash for his tweets, he blamed "right-wing nut-jobs" for the negative responses. He also wrote that all white people were responsible for slavery.

Bill Ayers, retired Distinguished Professor of Education and Senior Scholar at the University of Illinois at Chicago, was the leader of the violent "Weather Underground" group responsible for setting off bombs that destroyed government property and infrastructure. Of his group he said, "We are a guerrilla organization. We are communist women and men... deeply affected by the historic events of our time in the struggle against U.S. imperialism."

Bernardine Dohrn, a retired clinical associate professor of law at Northwestern University and Ayer's wife, was also a fugitive member of the Weather Underground, once making the FBI's top ten "Most Wanted" list. Recently she called for Cook County Jail to be turned into a public park. She envisions a world without jails.

> *Colleges are teaching students that if you disagree with a viewpoint, that viewpoint should be silenced. This is dangerous & wrong!*
>
> —*@charliekirk11, Apr. 12, 2017*

Dr. John Bellamy Foster, a psychology professor at the University of Oregon and editor of the Marxist magazine *Monthly Review*, advocates a "red-green" alliance to abolish capitalism and considers the collapse of the Soviet empire a setback for human progress.

Dr. John Griffin, Media Arts and Animation professor at the Art Institute of Washington, said Republicans "should be lined up and shot" over their vote to repeal Obamacare and pass a different healthcare reform bill. He also said, "Republicans are a f***ing joke and their voting bloc runs the gamut from monstrous to ignorant."

Dr. Kate Greene, an associate professor of Political Science at the University of Southern Mississippi, disrupted a conservative senator's lecture on campus organized by Pi Sigma Alpha, the university political science honor society.

Mark Tushnet, a law professor at Harvard University, asked liberals to begin treating Christians and conservatives like Nazis. In a blog post, he claimed that Christians and conservatives have lost, and the primary question now is "How to deal with the losers."

And, of course, let's not forget the infamous Melissa Click, the University of Missouri assistant communications professor, who was fired after interfering with journalists and police during student protests, calling for "some muscle" to remove a student videographer from a protest area. Not to worry for her, though: she got a new job with Gonzaga University as a lecturer in the undergraduate communication studies department.

We could go on and on. But I think that I've made my point. Read the rest at Professor Watchlist.

I get countless messages from students who say professors are lowering their grades and penalizing them for being conservative. As an aside, I posted that on Twitter, liberal journalist Jesse Farrar, an occasional contributor to Dead-spin and VICE Sports, tweeted that professors should "hold the conservative students [*sic*] heads under water until they stop breathing." I responded, "I'm sure he is joking, but imagine if conservatives made a joke like that against liberals?" Farrar wrote back "I am not joking," but later deleted the tweet. His Deadspin editor later wrote that Farrar was joking and said the organization "supports his stance of trolling white supremacist-minded" groups. As I later replied on "Fox & Friends," I was "stunned" by Farrar's comment. "They disagree with us so much and they're so bothered by our worldview and our viewpoint, that they literally want us dead. I hate playing the victim, but this is beyond the pale."

Of course, any discussion of liberal bias among professors awakens among them near fatal anguish, torment, and denial. One can only wonder how they would react if they found just one conservative professor making similar *ex cathedra* proclamations that America is the greatest country in history because of its historic commitment to liberty and capitalism.

First, it doesn't take extensive research to demonstrate that many, many professors are liberal, some of them extremely so. Granted, the above examples are anecdotal. But survey research backs it up.

Just one of many examples: Mitchell Langbert, Anthony J. Quain, and Daniel B. Klein, in an article published in *Econ Journal Watch*, said they checked out the voter registration of 7,243 teachers at forty leading U.S. universities. They found that 3,623 were registered Democrat and 314 Republican, for an overall Democrat to Republican ratio of

11.5-to-1. Democrats by far outnumbered Republicans in the five academic fields studied, with history professors recording the greatest disparity with 33.5 Democrats for every one Republican. The lowest ratio was, not surprisingly, economics, but Democrats there still outnumbered Republicans 4.5-to-1. Other ratios were journalism/communications, 20-to-1; law, 8.6-to-1; and psychology, 17.4-to-1.

The research also showed that the Democrat to Republican "ratios have increased since 2004, and the age profile suggests that in the future they will be even higher." They conclude that people concerned about the "errors of the leftist outlook—including students, parents, donors, and taxpayers—might find our results deeply troubling."

Indeed we do. Liberals have a tendency to downplay such results. So here are some more:

- More than 95 percent of political donations from University of Nebraska-Lincoln employees over three election cycles went to Democrats.

- Among the faculty, Democrats outnumbered Republicans 12-to-1 at the University of North Carolina. One professor there claimed that's because so many rank-and-file Republicans are "anti-science."

- The Cato 2017 Free Speech and Tolerance Survey found that only 20 percent of surveyed college and graduate students believe their faculty has a balanced mix of political views. A plurality of 39 percent say that most professors are liberal, 27 percent believe most are politically moderate, and a mere 12 percent believe most are conservative.

- The University of Colorado Boulder, realizing that most of its faculty are liberal, in 2013 launched a "bold experiment" to bring conservatives to its campus. The first, Steven Hayward, offended many by, among other things, mocking administrators who advise professors to address students according to their desired gender pronoun.

- In 2016, 93 percent of the 33.2 million dollars that all organized teachers' unions contributed to political campaigns went to Democrats.

Because the unions mostly represent K–12 teachers, we suspect that the trend isn't much different for high schools. At Rio Americano High School in Sacramento, California, a faculty survey and examination of voting records found that thirty-two were registered as Democrats, eight as Republicans, and the rest as others. Obviously, that's a tiny sample size that doesn't describe all American high schools, but can anyone find the opposite ratio in American public schools?

The left has to be blind not to notice this yawning gap. Or perhaps they're just deceiving themselves. Or they can't bring themselves to admit what is so obvious. In any case, the left is trying to avoid a reasonable discussion of the impact of this imbalance on their students or on the future of democracy.

Which brings us to liberals' second response to the fact that the left dominates the campus: "So what? Who cares? What difference does it make?"

Conservative students tell me it makes a lot of difference, in classroom discussion and their grades. Not that liberals want to find out what difference it makes. Researchers who should be most interested in this disparity—political scientists—have generally ignored it. So say April Kelly-Woessner of Elizabethtown College and Matthew C. Woessner of Penn State. They reported in *PS: Political Science and Politics,* a publication of the American Political Science Association, that they were surprised that political scientists have neglected to study how ideological differences affect the relationships between students and professors.

The researchers eloquently stated the importance of the "attitudinal" differences between the professor's and student's political ideology:

> In a classroom setting, students do not have the option of avoiding counter attitudinal statements. While we expect that students desire to maintain preexisting beliefs, they also wish to obtain good grades...and, hence, cannot skip classes or simply tune out professors' arguments. Unable to avoid counter attitudinal messages, students must either accept or attempt to discredit them. The first option may be difficult for the students if the message contradicts their deeply held views and personal values. Students may experience "cognitive dissonance" or discomfort as previously held convictions seem incompatible with new evidence. On the other hand, students may simply believe that their professors are incorrect and outright dismiss counter attitudinal claims.

Or put more frankly, the students might just decide their professors are full of it. As Christian Smith, a sociology professor at the University of Notre Dame, aptly put it in the Jan. 19, 2018 *Chronicle of Higher Education* under the headline "Higher education is drowning in BS. And it's mortally corrosive to society":

> BS is the grossly lopsided political ideology of the faculty of many disciplines, especially in the humanities and social sciences, creating a homogeneity of worldview to which those faculties are themselves oblivious, despite claiming to champion difference, diversity, and tolerance....

Smith is just getting started defining campus "BS": the "ascending culture of offense" that shuts down the "open exchange of ideas and mutual accountability to reason and argument," leading to "invisible self-censorship" and the "semi-intelligible outbursts of antagonism from enraged outsiders incited by academe's suppressions of open argument, which primarily work to validate and reinforce the self-assured superiority of the suppressors, and sometimes to silence other legitimate voices."

The problem isn't just that conservative students and liberal professors have different views. More importantly, the professors and the students are in what sociologists call a "power relationship," with the teacher able to punish the student in multiple ways, such as lowering grades, intimidation, isolation, exclusion, and humiliation. How ironic that liberals have correctly warned of how power can corrupt the relationship between male bosses and vulnerable female employees. Yet they neglect to study and appear unconcerned about that same kind of relationship between professor and student.

A host of studies have probed, as they should, how ethnicity, nationality, gender, and other attributes affect grading. But what does the research say about how being a conservative affects your grades? The liberal answer is that no research concludes that professors punish conservatives. But that's because virtually no credible research exists.

Liberals will point to a 2005 study of a single large public university, which concluded that conservative students received grades that were equal to or higher than their liberal counterparts. However, the methodology is faulty because it does not take into account students who swallow their beliefs and answer in the way they think their liberal professors want.

Social scientists, who are liberal to a fault, don't answer the question, but Turning Point USA is here to make sure that conservatives aren't punished in the classroom for their beliefs. That's why we compile the Professor Watchlist to identify the worst of the bunch. Curiously, many professors don't like to be listed and exposed, as if it isn't fair or constitutes an invitation to ridicule or worse. But these same professors have no problem with the standard practice of students grading their teachers on their colleges' websites.

Just as it takes honest and dedicated journalists to put aside their biases when reporting the news, college and even high school teachers need to commit to keeping their own biases out of the classroom. We admire those teachers who take a balanced and objective approach to scholarship in their classrooms. The classroom is supposed to be a sacred place where learning comes before propaganda and the search for truth supersedes brainwashing. But those who lace their lectures, tests, and required reading with their preferences are betraying their profession and their students.

And the faculty isn't the only source of suppression.

4

The Campus as a
Cloistered Convent

"Freedom of speech is something that represents the very dignity of what a human being is…. That's what marks us off from the stones and the stars. You can speak freely. It is almost impossible for me to describe. It is the thing that marks us as just below the angels."

Someone who valued free speech on the college campus spoke those words nearly a half-century ago. Mario Savio was a twenty-two-year-old liberal student leader of the historic Free Speech Movement that blossomed in 1964 on the campus of the University of California Berkeley and spread like wildfire on campuses throughout America. Savio and his activist students arrived on the scene just as the civil rights movement was reaching its peak and the protests against the Vietnam War were about to get seriously disruptive. Their fight for the right to assemble in peaceful protest, to campaign for social justice and equal opportunity for all, and for peace, was the bedrock of a great social movement that changed America in fundamental ways.

Today's students have betrayed that admirable legacy. They have shouted down invited speakers because their views are "hurtful." They pressure universities to cancel speakers they find "offensive." They demand that teachers issue "trigger warnings" in classrooms because some subject matter *might* stir discomfort in some students. They see nothing wrong with limiting free speech to a tiny slice of the campus in some far-off corner to avoid anyone stumbling upon something unpleasant. They praise speech codes that limit debate in, of all places, the academe—a place that Savio himself said is where scholars of all political persuasions can and ought to participate in free inquiry.

Savio made his goals clear: He was fighting against a school president, who as an "able practitioner of managerial tyranny," was seeking to make Berkeley a "knowledge factory." Savio told crowds of thousands of students that they were fighting for a "more traditional educational philosophy. We believe in a university of scholars and students with inquiry as its defining characteristic, and freedom as its fundamental tool."

Savio died in 1996, so it is hard to say how he would have reacted to how students on his old campus, the very birthplace of the free speech movement, violently disrupted a speech by right-wing firebrand Milo Yiannopoulos. How they tried to stamp "censored" on his speech before he gave it, so that some fellow students wouldn't be exposed to ideas and advocacy that are different from the currently "correct" favored ones.

> *Affirmative action is a racist program that punishes Asian Indian, and white students based on something they cannot control.*
>
> —@charliekirk11, April 19, 2018

Instead of shutting people up, at least in theory, Savio would have invited "offending" speakers to the university so he could publicly debate them. Such a debate would have a cleansing effect by exposing the depth of the rot underneath. Discomfort is the consequence of free speech, the kind of discomfort that leads to the confrontation of the given wisdom. In fact, confrontation was an integral part of Savio's protests. Many of his followers carried signs that prominently displayed the F-word precisely because it offended. As in "F... the draft." Considering how America was just emerging from the straight-laced 1950s, you can imagine how the sight of that vulgarity made some heads explode.

These were uneasy and contentious times. Jim Crow laws that confined African-Americans to the worst of public accommodations and squashed their voting rights were still on the books. School boycotts to protest school segregation were widely condemned. Public protest was considered radically instigated or "communist inspired." The Reverend Martin Luther King was told that he should cancel his marches in Chicago to support housing desegregation because they were provoking heated and sometimes violent reaction. King responded that he wouldn't relent because, if the reaction of people who objected to what was being said could be used to stop the speech, then the right of free speech was an empty promise.

Back then, much of Middle America thought precisely as the hard-left thinks today. Protest marches were condemned because, well, they offended so many people. Consider the role reversals. Savio and his self-described revolutionaries were on the left, some far on the left. Today, leftist students are calling for restrictions on free speech. Conservatives are fighting for more free speech. In this, conservatives are Savio's progeny. It is a great tragedy that this generation of students doesn't understand the significance of America's fight for free speech. The students who demand that conservative speakers, such as myself, be banned from campus have betrayed this honorable free speech tradition. After they leave college, they will poison society with their own disrespect of free speech and individual liberty.

The sad and frightening part is that many of the attacks come from fellow students. Distinguished political science professor Donald Downs of the University of Wisconsin-Madison has concluded that today's collective student body is behaving badly, increasingly so. "Today's suppression differs from the previous era in three key aspects: it is more passionate and aggressive; it is more student-initiated and driven; and it extends the reach of censorship more deeply into everyday campus life and the life of the mind," according to his post on the website of the James G. Martin Center for Academic Renewal.

Students wield their power in several ways. First, they have been successful in intimidating the administration into issuing directives about trigger warnings, microaggressions, free speech zones, and so forth. Second, students have a formidable tool: peer pressure. It includes shunning, intimidation, scolding, and the threat of or actual violence against fellow students.

> *The left needs people to be victims. As soon as they become VICTORS their entire political plot and agenda crumbles We believe in the power of the individual to rise above government welfare and dependence The left needs people to need them Don't be a victim, be a victor.*
>
> —*@charliekirk11, May 7, 2018*

There are way too many incidents to list here, popping up as they do nearly every day: From ripping down posters advertising conservative causes and speakers to erasing conservative messages on sidewalks written in chalk. And assaults.

Here's a recent one:

A Dartmouth student, Ryan Spector, wrote an op-ed in *The Dartmouth* school newspaper arguing that bias, rather than merit, determined the selection of upperclassmen hosts for the school's Outing Club "trips" to introduce freshmen to college life. In his article "You're Not Tripping," Spector noted that the school hires five female hostesses for every male host. He argued that the gender disparity on the directorate that picks the hosts—of the nineteen members, fifteen are female—was the result of a selection process "that sees race, gender and identity as dictating qualifications" despite purportedly being "purely based on merit."

College Fix reported that the condemnations of Spector were fulsome and not long in coming. His words were defined as "violent" by several campus groups and ignited calls that he and the newspaper be punished for printing the piece. The Foundation for Individual Rights in Education fleshed out the details:

> ...30 campus organizations denounced him, many calling his piece an "attack" on women and other minority groups. Several student organizations claimed the piece "endangers the lives" of students and suggested that his fraternity discipline him or dissociate from his views. Others lamented "how violent this article is" and urged The Dartmouth to retract the piece and apologize for "sacrific[ing] the safety and well-being of students."
>
> While many clubs expressed good-faith disagreements with Spector's arguments, several accused Spector and The Dartmouth of committing violence. As stated by one of Spector's detractors when calling on Spector's fraternity to condemn his op-ed: "[W]e call upon Alpha Chi Alpha to acknowledge that their own words do not recognize that their brother has committed an act of violence."

The obvious question: If someone had written an op-ed accusing a campus organization of favoring men over women in the selection of hosts, would that be an act of "violence"? Of course not. That's because this is just one example of the hypocritical double standard that grips so many American campuses.

Speaking of violence, let us now turn to Middlebury College, a Vermont liberal arts school with about 2,500 students. There, a teacher was hospitalized for a neck injury caused by a mob protesting the appearance of a conservative speaker, Charles Murray. (Never mind that many of the protestors had not read his 1994 book, *The Bell Curve: Intelligence and Class Structure in American Life*, which protestors cited as the reason to block his appearance.)

Before Murray began speaking, Middlebury President Laurie L. Patton eloquently asked the students to listen closely and then engage Murray:

> ...[I]f there ever was a time for Americans to take on arguments that offend us, it is now. If there ever was a time for us to challenge influential public views with better reason, better research, better logic, and better data, it is now. If there ever was a time when we need to argue back, to declare ourselves committed to arguing for a better society, it is now.

Her challenge fell on deaf ears. Shortly after he began to speak, large sections of the audience stood, turned their backs on Murray and shouted a speech of their own.

Professor Allison Stanger, a Democrat who had agreed to participate in the event and was sympathetic to hearing what Murray had to say, took up the story on her Facebook page:

I want you to know what it feels like to look out at a sea of students yelling obscenities at other members of my beloved community. There were students and faculty who wanted to hear the exchange, but were unable to do so, either because of the screaming and chanting and chair pounding in the room, or because their seats were occupied by those who refused to listen, and they were stranded outside the doors. I saw some of my faculty colleagues who had publicly acknowledged that they had not read anything Dr. Murray had written join the effort to shut down the lecture. All of this was deeply unsettling to me. What alarmed me most, however, was what I saw in student eyes from up on that stage. Those who wanted the event to take place made eye contact with me. Those intent on disrupting it steadfastly refused to do so. It was clear to me that *they had effectively dehumanized me.* They couldn't look me in the eye, because if they had, they would have seen another human being. There is a lot to be angry about in America today, but nothing good ever comes from demonizing our brothers and sisters. [Emphasis added.]

Murray, with the help of some faculty who still thought that college is a place of higher education, tried to speak elsewhere on campus, but he literally was driven away. True to form, the protestors claimed that they were the victims.

Broadly speaking, that's hardly so. Middlebury's students are among America's richest and most privileged. The annual cost to attend is nearly sixty-four thousand dollars a year, but that shouldn't be a problem for most—the average student comes from a household that makes two hundred and fifty thousand dollars a year. Twenty-three percent are members of that often-derided top one percent.

Can you imagine what these anti-democratic students would do if you gave them formal powers? You don't have to imagine; it happened at University of Wisconsin-Stevens Point where the school's student government voted unanimously to deny recognition to a chapter of Turning Point USA. This was after other students threatened Emily Strangeld, the chapter leader, hoping that they could frighten her into disbanding the club.

> *School in CA has graphic mural depicting the President being killed by an Aztec warrior. Zero outrage from the mainstream press. If an artist distastefully depicted Obama like this there would be protests in the streets. The left no longer just hates Trump. They want him dead.*
>
> *—@charliekirk11, Feb 3, 2017*

So, it was ironic that opponents of the chapter called it the threat. For three hours, the student government heard accusations that Turning Point encouraged hate speech on line. Lyn Ciurro, a transgender student, said members of marginalized groups would not feel "safe" if the chapter was officially recognized. "They would be more likely to not return to school if they knew organizations like these were accepted and are now part of the UW culture," Ciurro said. Reassurances that the chapter and Turning Point itself are dedicated to free speech, capitalism, and limited government were to no avail. And I'll reiterate: we do not discriminate.

Recognizing that case law forbids a publicly funded university from discriminating on the basis of political beliefs, the university had no choice but to overturn the student government's ban. Al Thompson, vice chancellor for student affairs, issued the bad news to the narrow-minded student government:

> I asked [the student government] to reconsider its action on November 16, based on UW-Stevens Point and UW System policies recognizing student organizations, SGA guidelines on viewpoint neutrality and a UW Board of Regents policy on academic expression. In the absence of further SGA action on November 16, I have determined that Turning Point USA meets the requirements to be recognized as a student organization at UW-Stevens Point.
>
> As an institution that values diversity and the freedom to explore all ideas, even unpopular ones, UW-Stevens Point remains committed to a learning environment that respects multiple viewpoints and ensures discourse is civil and our campus is safe for all.

If the school were a respectful learning environment, how do you explain that the student government was allowed to go as far as banning an organization that had a *prima facie* right to exist? Thompson told the *Washington Examiner* that the episode was "a learning experience," adding, "We are a learning environment, and if a university cannot have this dialogue, where can you have it?"

Precisely. It was a learning experience for both the students and the administration. Put the students in charge and you will have universities popping up all across the land where dialogue is not possible. Our Midwest regional manager, Timon Prax, summed it up for the *Washington Examiner*: "This sets a great precedent among conservative college students nationwide with beliefs perceived as unpopular on campus. If campuses judge ideas by how popular they are—students aren't being exposed to diverse thought—the ultimate mission of higher education."

We should not be surprised that the campus is becoming more like a cloistered convent than an arena for intellectual debate. Look at the mistaken views that some have of the First Amendment. According to John Villasenor, a nonresident senior fellow in Governance Studies and the Center for Technology Innovation at the Brookings Institute,

> ...many students have an overly narrow view of the extent of freedom of expression. For example, a very significant percentage of students hold the view that hate speech is unprotected. In addition, a surprisingly large fraction of students believe it is acceptable to act—including resorting to violence—to shut down expression they consider offensive. And a majority of students appear to want an environment that shields them from being exposed to views they might find offensive.

How frightening is that?

Villasenor draws his conclusion from a survey of 1,500 undergraduate students at U.S. four-year colleges and universities. Here are some details:

Hate speech: As we've seen, significant numbers (44 percent) of students believe that the U.S. Constitution—namely the First Amendment—does not protect hate speech. Thus, they believe they are within their rights to demand that hate speech be silenced.

But it is protected. Only 39 percent correctly answered. The survey uncovered a significant difference between men and women. Fifty-one percent of men correctly said that hate speech is protected, compared with 31 percent of women.

Controversial speaker: Is it all right to shout down an offensive speaker so others cannot hear him? A slight majority (51 percent) agreed that it is. Democrats, by a wide margin compared with Republicans (62 percent to 39 percent), agree. Democrats of old, the kind who contributed to the American Civil Liberties Union, would be appalled. Shouting down a speaker clearly is not the intent of the First Amendment.

Counter point: A large majority believes that the First Amendment requires that an opposing view be presented alongside the offensive speaker. As fair as that might be, the First Amendment does not require the appearance of opposing views.

Learning environment: The survey asked what kind of learning environment the students preferred: A positive one in which there are no "speech or expression of viewpoints that are offensive or biased against certain groups of people" or an "open learning environment [in which] students are exposed to all types of speech and viewpoints, even if it means allowing speech that is offensive or biased against certain groups of people."

A majority (53 percent to 47 percent) chose a comfortable surrounding over a challenging environment. Democrats chose a sheltered environment by a wide margin over Republicans—61 percent to 47 percent.

Villasenor concludes:

The survey results establish with data what has been clear anecdotally to anyone who has been observing campus dynamics in recent years: Freedom of expression is deeply imperiled on U.S. campuses. In fact, despite protestations to the contrary (often with statements like "we fully support the First Amendment, but..."), freedom of expression is clearly not, in practice, available on many campuses, including many public campuses that have First Amendment obligations.

Despite some flaws in the methodology (e.g., the respondents were not a random sample), the anecdotal evidence cannot be ignored. Incident after incident in which hostile students trash the guarantee of free speech are readily available.

Too many students today clearly don't understand the First Amendment freedoms and the idea of a university. It is disturbing to know that significant numbers of students in all categories, even if not a plurality, had a perverted view of free speech and higher education. Do students enter the college setting expecting a sheltered environment because, well, they always have been sheltered? Or is it something they learn in college from their teachers?

Are they taught that the diversity of physical appearance and background far outweighs the presence of a diversity of opinions and beliefs? Let's see.

5

A Pillow for Your Thoughts

Colleges fawn over "diversity," pledging their whole heart and soul to the cause of ensuring that their campuses "include" everyone. They appoint directors of diversity, schedule diversity seminars, fill their freshmen orientation with a parade of "change agents" to awaken white guilt, and bend the curriculum toward courses that "raise awareness" of the need to enfold all persons who fit every racial, gender, ethnic, cultural, sexual orientation, and other "excluded" descriptors.

Notably absent from their idea of inclusion, however, are conservatives. Inclusion for so many colleges does not mean tolerating or welcoming anything that does not pass the muster of the liberal inclusion patrols. Inclusion only admits into the sacred circle the products of liberal, progressive, or socialist thinking. Colleges claim the high ground of inclusion, but it's only lip service. Only liberal views are worthy of being fostered and nurtured. It is high-level hypocrisy.

How has this happened?

Because higher education administrators have allowed it to happen. Some have encouraged it to happen. These administrators have knifed the very idea of a university handed down through the centuries by deans and dons. Colleges are supposed to be a place of discourse, characterized by thoughtful debate, a search for knowledge, and civility. The substance of the discourse is supposed to prevail over who speaks it. The ideal was well expressed by John Stuart Mill in his *On Liberty,* where he argued that free and open discussion is a necessary ingredient of human progress in science, arts, and the human condition.

> *Our colleges are creating a generation of young people looking around waiting to be offended by something.*
> —@charliekirk11, May 8, 2018

One of the best understandings of a university I've seen comes from Amy Wax, the Robert Mundheim Professor of Law at the University of Pennsylvania Law School. In an essay in the *Wall Street Journal,* she called civil discourse, "the sine qua non of liberal education and democracy." She said:

Democracy thrives on talk and debate, and it is not for the faint of heart. I read things every day in the media and hear things every day at my job that I find exasperating and insulting, including falsehoods and half-truths about people who are my friends. Offense and upset go with the territory; they are part and parcel of an open society. We should be teaching our young people to get used to these things, but instead we are teaching them the opposite.

Disliking, avoiding and shunning people who don't share our politics is not good for our country. We live together, and we need to solve our problems together. It is also always possible that people we disagree with have something to offer, something to contribute, something to teach us. We ignore this at our peril.

Alas, Wax knew what she was talking about because she was shunned and worse for co-authoring with Larry Alexander, of the University of San Diego Law School, an op-ed called "Paying the Price for the Breakdown of the Country's Bourgeois Culture" that appeared in the *Philadelphia Inquirer*. In it, they found that some of the virtues of the so-called bourgeois culture of the 1950s might have some curative impact on today's problems. Thus she speaks highly of marriage; children born and raised in wedlock; respect for authority; and loyalty to employer and country.

Gasp. How dare she?

The nasty emails rolled in, characterized by name-calling and absent any discussion of the merits of what she's saying. They scourged her for her wanting to drag everyone back to the 1950s when Jim Crow was prowling the land and women were assigned only to housewifely duties. Half the law school faculty wrote a scolding open letter. Shame, shame. All of this, as expected. My point here is something more: She failed to receive backing from the school's administration, defending her right to present what is, after all, a legitimate and reasoned argument.

A deputy dean joined the scolding, indicating she would have signed the public flogging letter but couldn't because of her "official position." Nonetheless, she called the letter "necessary" to get Wax's attention, so that she would "rethink" her position and contemplate the hurt and damage she had caused. The message was clear, Wax said: "Cease the heresy."

Meanwhile, the calls for someone to do something to make Wax's life miserable continued. Her account:

> My law school dean recently asked me to take a leave of absence next year and to cease teaching a mandatory first-year course. He explained that he was getting "pressure" to banish me for my unpopular views and hoped that my departure would quell the controversy. When I suggested that it was his job as a leader to resist such illiberal demands, he explained that he is a "pluralistic dean" who must listen to and accommodate "all sides."

In other words, the administration threw Wax to the wolves.

What the hell is a "pluralistic dean?" If he were truly pluralist, he would defend and advance everyone's right to not just have an opinion, but also to express it freely on campus without nasty repercussions. It's hard to tell how many times college administrators have similarly abetted the close-minded; it's certainly not advertised and it takes a lot of courage for the target of the vendetta to expose it.

Instead of sticking up for free speech and association on campus, as is their duty, many college administrations across the country have created every imaginable dodge to facilitate the illiberal—safe spaces, trigger warnings, micro-aggressions and, ironically, free speech codes.

Too often, an administration's commitment to free speech is simply lip service or, worse, a camouflage for inviting liberals to take the stage while muzzling conservatives. Free speech codes are nothing more than a college administration's creation of a cover for limiting the speech of a few. Some schools, more sensitive to the charge that free speech codes actually suppress speech, have slyly renamed them hate speech codes. Those schools argue that the hurt feelings that those codes prevent are more important than the First Amendment right of free speech. Granted, no right is absolute, but when hurt feelings are used as an excuse to get in the way of a constitutional right, then something is wrong.

Kentucky State University, for example, added "embarrassment" to the list of definitions (e.g. abuse and harassment) on its list of prohibited "offenses against persons." In other words, making someone "uncomfortably self-conscious"—the dictionary definition of "embarrass"—is prohibited speech.

At Harvard University, the administration seems determined not just to choke free speech, but also freedom of association, also a First Amendment right. It is banning members of independent, single-sex, off-campus organizations from receiving Rhodes and Marshall scholarships and from leadership roles of on-campus organizations or athletic teams. The goal of this vast overreach affecting single-sex fraternities and sororities, as well as all-male "final" clubs, is to foster "inclusion" and "address deeply rooted gender attitudes," said Harvard President Drew Gilpin Faust.

> *People who fought & fled socialism are now seeing their grandkids go to college and learn to advocate bringing it here.*
>
> —*@charliekirk11, Sept. 17, 2017*

Garbage. It is an attempt to punish fraternities and clubs for their maleness by turning them into gender-neutral clubs. All female sororities will just have to go along with it. Fraught with legal, constitutional, and practical problems (e.g. the membership in the final clubs is secret), the administration's ban amounts to a blackjacking of college students to accept the faddish left-wing dictum that gender "assignment" is "arbitrary." In a feeble-minded attempt to create "diversity," it is imposing uniformity. For that, FIRE, the Foundation for Individual Rights in Education, named Harvard—for the fourth year in a row—to its list of the 10 Worst Colleges for Free Speech, 2018.

Also on the list of worst offenders is Evergreen State College in Olympia, Washington for a truly cockamamie idea in the first place. Each year, the college staff holds a "Day of Absence," when people of color leave campus to demonstrate how much the school needs them. But in 2017, the administration decided to ask white people to leave instead. Biology Professor Bret Weinstein reasonably criticized the idea on a staff and faculty email list as exclusionary, based on skin color. That provoked a response from about fifty students who disrupted his class with shouts of "racist" and chants that drowned him out when he tried to speak. When he tried to leave, they blocked his way. Because Weinstein and his wife, also a professor, were unable to return safely to campus, they left their jobs. The episode cost the school a five-hundred-thousand-dollar settlement.

New on the 2018 list is the Lifetime Censorship Award recognizing a school as the worst of the worst schools for free speech. It went to DePaul University in Chicago for a series of repressions going back to 2005, when the school banned posters criticizing controversial professor Ward Churchill. Among its other offenses: charging a student group with harassment for an event satirizing affirmative action; denying recognition to a student group criticizing marijuana laws; tagging a student with conduct violations for identifying students who had vandalized its campus pro-life display; and requiring a student group to pay for security guards during an appearance by a controversial speaker. The school also forbade a student group from using the promotional slogan, "Gay lives matter" because it would "be co-opting another movements [sic] approach."

Just how pitiful a college administration can be was on display at San Diego State University, where students were provided with a "healing circle" to help them process their "confusion, anger and fear over Donald Trump's election and develop ways to stand against injustice," reported the *College Fix*. It was held under the auspices of...wait for it...San Diego State's College of Education's Counseling and School Psychology Department's Minor in Counseling and Social Change. How sweet. Can you imagine the school sponsoring pity parties for conservative students troubled by the election of Barack Obama as president?

I could go on. But suffice it to say that a school's leadership has an important role, not just to protect free speech, but also to promote it. How can anyone expect students to understand the importance of free speech when so many colleges are working against open dialogue?

Fortunately, we have a model of how a university should approach the subject. That would be the University of Chicago, where Dean of Students John Ellison told incoming freshmen in a letter that they're not heading for a soft bed and pillow where they could cuddle up, their opinions safe and sound, never to be challenged. He laid it on the line:

> Our commitment to academic freedom means that we do not support so-called "trigger warnings," we do not cancel invited speakers because their topics might prove controversial, and we do not condone the creation of intellectual "safe spaces" where individuals can retreat from ideas and perspectives at odds with their own.

The letter linked to a statement from the school's Committee on Freedom of Expression:

> It is not the proper role of the University to attempt to shield individuals from ideas and opinions they find unwelcome, disagreeable, or even deeply offensive. Although the University greatly values civility, and although all members of the University community share in the responsibility for maintaining a climate of mutual respect, concerns about civility and mutual respect can never be used as a justification for closing off discussion of ideas, however offensive or disagreeable those ideas may be to some members of our community.

Dwell on the word "never." As in: concerns about civility and mutual respect can never, ever, trump free discussion, however offensive. The University of Chicago fully understands what it is about. It has long been a place of superior scholarship and learning precisely because it explores, dissects and questions. And the last I saw, the university did not collapse into a heap of self-pity and hurt feelings.

6

Safe Spaces Suck

For liberals, the entire college campus is a safe space. They can call conservatives anything they want. Without criticism. Without penalty. Without rebuke, official or otherwise. Fascist! Bigot! Homophobe! Racist! Birther! Misogynist! Wingnut! Oh, and let's not forget: Deplorable!

So, why aren't conservatives falling in line with put-upon liberals to demand safe spaces to relieve themselves from the stresses of being an intellectual and political minority on campus? After all, if there's a frenzied drive to provide safe spaces for liberals, why not for conservatives, too?

I could think of a lot of reasons. Such as, conservatives don't live in a liberal fantasy world where they are taken care of by cadres of compassionate folks who feel their hurt. Or this: The need for safe spaces reflects and is a part of the "politics of identity"—something that conservatives find so abhorrent. Or that the mission of so many universities has been sidetracked from education to social activism, of which safe spaces is a part.

Ask a liberal why conservatives aren't demanding their own safe spaces and you'll be told that conservatives aren't a "historically marginalized group." As if marginalizing conservatives now is perfectly okay.

No matter. We're here to analyze why safe spaces have become such an imperative for true believers. And why they pose a danger.

Defining a "safe space" can be difficult because there seem to be as many versions as there are colleges that have bent to the demands to create them. Generally, we're talking about physical places where the victimized can go to be walled off from any form of harassment, including hurt feelings. Their goal is to stomp out any "profound feelings of discomfort" on the part of "target groups." Safe spaces are a favored tool for bringing "social justice" and "positive learning environments" to the campus. They are based on the unrealistic assumption that the best way to learn about social justice is to reject diverse viewpoints, namely ones that you don't agree with. That true solutions can be best found in an atmosphere free from criticism and conflict, or anything that even hints of disagreements.

For some, it is an "autonomous area" with codes of conduct, not necessarily written, that proscribe certain speech or any other actions that would make someone feel unwelcome. They provide an "inclusive environment" for members of the lesbian, gay, bisexual, transgender and questioning (LGBTQ) community. For women too. And African Americans. Also for a "Trans*gressive genderqueer Latinx" according to one person who "...embraces living on the border of fe/male and the constant crossing over and disruption of normative masculinity." (Latinx is a gender-neutral alternative to Latino and Latina.)

UC Irvine Black Students at the University of California-Irvine demanded the creation of a Black Scholars' Hall—"a safe space where Black history, culture, and intellectual thought is celebrated."

Concordia College in Moorhead, Minnesota aims to make its entire campus a safe space. At Claremont Colleges in Claremont, California, a student newspaper is setting aside some of its columns for "unfiltered safe space" where "people of color" can voice their experiences. The University of California at Berkeley has something called an Ace Space program that provides comfort for, among others, South Asian LGBTQIA students, staff, and faculty. ("I" is for intersex and "A" is for asexual or ally.)

Allies of LGBTQ youth can show their support by ordering a Safe Space Kit that lets them assess the school's climate and "strategize" change. The package includes stickers and posters so the victimized will know when they're in a safe space.

At Texas A&M University-San Antonio, a safe space is not a place, nor an office or a department. It's a *person* "who provides a safe space that is highly visible and easily identifiable to the LGBTQ+ community. A Safe Space is where support and understanding are key and bigotry and discrimination are not tolerated." You become a safe space by attending workshops, after which you get a "Safe Space certificate" to show, I suppose, that you are a trained, compassionate person.

Some activists want to expand safe spaces to dormitories, creating, for example, all-black buildings. For people who lived through the fight for civil rights, it's a stunning regression back to Jim Crow and legal racial segregation. It should be the same for inclusion activists today, but for some reason they aren't bothered by this kind of exclusion.

How this leftist escapism took root is lost in the fog of time. One school of thought is that it began with 1960s and 1970s feminism, when women sought to create a community of people with shared interests who were fighting for their rights. It was a gender-based movement that morphed through gay liberation activism and into the current contentious atmosphere of gender identification. Another school of thought argues that it began decades before in corporate "sensitivity training," in which employees were allowed to speak honestly without fear of ridicule or retaliation.

All with good motives, to be sure. But the safe spaces vogue creates a quandary that doesn't bode well for the preservation of vibrant universities or for those who are supposed to benefit. Or, ultimately, for America.

In a *Washington Post* op-ed, Morton Schapiro, president of Northwestern University, touched on the quandary as he sympathized with students wanting a safe place. He illustrated his point with this story:

> A group of black students were having lunch together
> in a campus dining hall. There were a couple of empty
> seats, and two white students asked if they could join

them. One of the black students asked why, in light of empty tables nearby. The reply was that these students wanted to stretch themselves by engaging in the kind of uncomfortable learning the college encourages. The black students politely said no. Is this really so scandalous?...

We all deserve safe spaces. Those black students had every right to enjoy their lunches in peace. There are plenty of times and places to engage in uncomfortable learning, but that wasn't one of them. The white students, while well meaning, didn't have the right to unilaterally decide when uncomfortable learning would take place.

More to my point, Schapiro poses one of the great ironies of the safe space movement:

...[E]xperts tell me that students don't fully embrace uncomfortable learning unless they are themselves comfortable. Safe spaces provide that comfort. The irony, it seems, is that the *best hope we have of creating an inclusive community is to first create spaces where members of each group feel safe.* [Emphasis added.]

Well yes, we all seek places of comfort where we can find like-minded people and familiar surroundings. But what we have in the safe space frenzy is a fundamental change in the value that used to be called integration. It turns on its head the idea that we learn by living together, working together, worshipping together, partying together, and raising our children together. Among old time liberals, integration was an article of faith. Now that very idea is under attack by liberals themselves. That we can learn to be inclusive by first becoming exclusive is an idea that is at war with itself.

> *Is this who you want teaching your kids? Professor at John Jay college says "it's a privilege to be able to teach future dead cops."*
> —@charliekirk11, Sept. 15, 2017

Laws were passed and legal rulings were handed down supporting the incorporation of integration into the mainstream culture. For example, the Supreme Court in its unanimous *Brown v. Board of Education of Topeka* ruling in 1954 declared that "separate but equal" public schools for black and white students were unconstitutional. It was a bombshell decision that overturned the *Plessy v. Ferguson* decision of 1896 that allowed segregation in public schools.

Integration was about more than "desegregation." Integration was premised on the idea that if we can get to know one another better, we can all live together better. Open housing laws that outlawed residential segregation, for example, are based on the idea that whites can learn from blacks and blacks from whites. Class integration is when low-income families learn the values and practices that will raise them out of poverty by coming to live in successful communities. In Chicago, the issue played out in decades of court cases that forced the destruction of huge concentrations of high-rise public housing, occupied by poor, black families. Following the integration model, they were relocated in "scattered site housing" throughout the metropolitan area. Integration was a major plank in the liberal platform.

Liberals continue to give lip-service support to integration. Yet, their devotion has been softened by the identity politics and Marxist class warfare battles that now are standard pillars of liberal ideology. Even the suggestion that blacks can learn from whites and whites from blacks, or the poor can learn from the successful ignites charges of racism, classism and all the other isms of the "progressive" agenda.

When it comes down to it, Americans cherish togetherness. They form groups based on common interests. Black churches, veteran organizations, bridge groups, curling clubs and a host of other events and activities that bring us together are an important part of our culture. Golfers like to have a beer in the clubhouse after a round of golf. Bowlers gather to brag about their games, most likely boring anyone who doesn't want to talk about the sport. It's why, despite open housing laws, ethnic groups tend to prefer to gravitate to the same neighborhoods.

This is called freedom of association, also protected under the First Amendment. If people of like mind want to get together in an atmosphere of sameness, that is their right. Indeed, no one wants to outlaw safe spaces on campus. They perform an important function, whether it is letting off steam about how you're being treated or discussing ways to move forward.

However, the problem with the safe space movement on campus comes when it elbows out or diminishes the importance of higher education's essential mission: when a comfortable atmosphere becomes more important than the clash of ideas and open debate. Debate is supposed to be conducted civilly. When clashes do go beyond civil, the solution is not to retreat into a cocoon, but to reengage civilly. That is why, at Turning Point USA, civility and respect are as much a part of our approach as is a command of facts.

Safe spaces by themselves do nothing to prepare students for the real world they will encounter after college. They poorly prepare students for the give-and-take that's a part of that world. Worse, if safe spaces become nothing more than wallowing in self-pity, they become a real danger. And if the safe space philosophy of retreating from the difficult by fleeing into a bubble of self-absorption takes hold of the entire campus, then we're all in trouble.

The rough-and-tumble of energetic debate are the tools of a successful democracy. If we end up hiding, each in our emotional stronghold, nothing gets done. No mutual understanding is reached. Solutions to our vexing social and economic challenges become orphans.

7

"Sticks and Stones May Break My Bones..."

But words will never hurt me.

Oh, but they will, if you're attending any number of American universities today. Words have become sticks and stones. Actually worse. They can hurt your sensitivities. Wreck your self-esteem. Offend your feelings. Make you feel rotten. Insult your heritage. Deny your worth. Send you into a depressive funk. And so much more.

Words now are microaggressions, the endless slights, snubs, rebuffs, and low-blows, whether intentional or not, that have sucked this generation of Americans into the deepest recesses of self-sympathy. Students, faculty, and administrators have become so overly sensitized to slights and innocent off-handed remarks that colleges have morphed from places of higher learning into playgrounds where name-calling sends children home crying.

Now, instead of "words can never hurt me," we have the dictum that "words have power," or as life coach Hyder Zahed said in the *Huffington Post*, "Words are singularly the most powerful force available to humanity," apparently believing they can flatten cities and move mountains.

Colleges are so obsessed with microaggressions that they have obscured the true mission of higher education. How could this happen?

The word microaggression was coined by Harvard University psychiatrist Chester Pierce in 1970 to describe frequent and casual remarks that put down African Americans and later any "marginalized" group—women, gays, Hispanics, and immigrants. Psychologist Derald Wing Sue later expanded the definition to include "brief, everyday exchanges that send denigrating messages to certain individuals because of their group membership." Others observe that instances of microaggressions pile up over time, leading to a major crisis. They usually arise from bias about a person's race, sex, sexual orientation, disability, religion, class, ethnicity, or any other newly discovered marginalized victims of the dominant society.

The American Psychological Association added more complexity to the term: "Some racism is so subtle that neither victim nor perpetrator may entirely understand what is going on—which may be especially toxic for people of color." And so, clearly both victim and victimizer need to be educated about the evils of microaggressions. Psychologist Sue is busily itemizing and classifying insults to help people of color understand when they are being marginalized and to let the aggressors know when they have crossed the red line. "It's a monumental task," he said, "to get white people to realize that they are delivering microaggressions, because it's scary to them. It assails their self-image of being good, moral, decent human beings to realize that maybe at an unconscious level they have biased thoughts, attitudes and feelings that harm people of color."

And maybe, at the unconscious level, the researcher's poor self-image blinds him to the damage he's doing to everyone by creating conflict when little or none exists. See how dangerous assumptions like that can so easily become a part of the discussion?

Now the catch-all term has been found to be so useful to intimidate people you don't like that it has been expanded to a dizzying vocabulary of words so extensive that no one knows the complete list. Yet, anyone who accidentally or unknowingly speaks such words is ipso facto guilty of an aggression, which means maybe it's time for him to "check his privilege."

Where do we start on the list? The University of Wisconsin-Milwaukee went straight to the point by adding to its official list of no-noes the phrase "politically incorrect" as a micro-aggressive "dismissive term." No surprise there.

> *Every college socialist should be encouraged to live under a Marxist regime for 6 months.*
> *Would love to see the Bernie bros try and survive in Venezuela without running water, food, shelter, or wifi. Socialism sounds great till it kills you and your family.*
>
> —*@charliekirk11 Jan. 22, 2018*

But is it racist to ask someone "Where are you from?" It used to be a conversation starter, but now it's a microaggression because it suggests that the question is directed at someone who is an outsider, who doesn't belong here, or who isn't as good as the asker.

Thanks go to the American Psychologist for elaborating on the list. For example, it's a microaggression to say, "You speak good English." Or ask an Asian American to teach them words in their native language. Asking once implied curiosity and interest in a foreign culture; no more.

Don't ask an Asian person to help with a math or science problem because it assumes that all Asians are good in math and science. Even though an Asian classmate is actually good at solving math problems, and you need help understanding them.

"When I look at you, I don't see color," amounts to denying a person of color's racial experiences. Never mind that it once was a term of endearment, meaning, "when I look at you, I see the things that make you a person, not a skin color." A good example of how no good intention goes unpunished.

Here's another microaggression: A white man or woman clutching their purse or checking their wallet as a black or Latino approaches or passes. It presumes that people of color are dangerous, criminal or deviant on the basis of their race. Of course, some people are just naturally cautious and respond like that whenever a stranger of any color approaches, but they still get counted among those slinging about microaggressions.

"I'm not a racist. I have several black friends," is a cliché that has faded from use as proof that you aren't a racist. The expression has been so ridiculed that only the most unthinking would make it. Of course, there's the possibility that it's true the speaker has black friends and isn't a racist.

In an attack on meritocracy, these observations are classified as racist microaggressions: "I believe the most qualified person should get the job." And, "Everyone can succeed in this society, if they work hard enough." Yes, it's true that some people take such criticism personally, especially if they are unemployed. But the statements also are true, an underpinning of the conservative movement.

According to others, here are more microaggressions: In the classroom, assuming the gender of any student and misusing personal pronouns even after a student, transgender or not, indicates his/her preference. Telling your wife that she looks great for a grandma. Telling a date that he looks nice, kind of feminine. A professor citing as a source more men than women. Having "male" or "female" on employee application forms; it forces the applicant to pick between the two. Golf outings. A teacher fails to call on non-white students often enough. The academic calendar arranged around religious holidays, making Christmas vacation a microaggression. The words "boyfriend," "girlfriend," "husband," and "wife" because it creates "the expectation that people do not identify as LGBTQ until they say otherwise or disclose their sexual orientation." Instead you should say the neutered "partner" or "spouse."

Among the banished expressions are: "Those people," "I don't like short hair on girls," "Please stand and be recognized,"

"I love your shoes," "We are all human beings," "All lives matter," "America is a melting pot," and "mankind."

Those who hunger for more of this gruel can visit a website devoted exclusively to microaggressions at microaggressions.com where you can learn the difference between micro-assaults, micro-insults and micro-invalidations. While exploring the minefields of such micros, I came across a question that illustrates the confusion over microaggressions: A writer asks whether, as a non-Muslim white person, he can add a blog post about a microaggression relating to Islamophobia at his Christian church. It took some two hundred words to answer: No. The unabridged version: "While you clearly are conscious and recognize the Islamophobic micro-aggression, [this] project is about providing a voice for people who have to experience it." The blog responder didn't infer it, but if I were leftist through-and-through, I would say that someone posting about something that he himself didn't experience is a microaggression itself—a "cultural misappropriation." But that's a story for another time.

Back to examples of microaggressions:

A "cultural competency workshop" at the University of North Carolina informs white people they are privileged because they can buy Band-Aids "in 'flesh' color" and have "them more or less match their vaguely beige-hued skin."

The Lily, which is published by the *The Washington Post*, described the devastating microaggression experienced by Arum Kang, co-founder of dating app Coffee Meets Bagel, while pitching her company: "I became painfully aware this year that the questions that I mostly receive from these male investors are focused on potential losses ('How predictable are your future cash flows?'), whereas men get asked promotional questions ('What are your next big milestones?'). I've also flat-out been asked how old I was. Now that I have a child, I get asked questions about work-life balance. I used to have my baby's photo [as a background] on my phone. Not anymore." Err, aren't questions about cash flow sort of essential for potential investors?

Here's another instance, described in *The Atlantic*:

Last fall at Oberlin College, a talk held as part of Latino Heritage Month was scheduled on the same evening that intramural soccer games were held. As a result, soccer players communicated by email about their respective plans. "Hey, that talk looks pretty great," a white student wrote to a Hispanic student, "but on the off chance you aren't going or would rather play futbol instead the club team wants to go!!"

I'm not quite sure exactly what the student was trying to stay, but according to the blast he received back, his message was chock full of insults and micro-aggressions. It said:

Ok. 1. Thanks for you thinking that the talk is "pretty great." I appreciate your white male validation. I see that it isn't interesting enough for you to actually take your ass to the talk. 2. Who said it was ok for you to say futbol? It's Latino Heritage Month, you're telling people not to come to the talk, but want to use our language? Trick NO! White students appropriating the Spanish language, dropping it in when convenient, never ok. Keep my heritage language out your mouth!

If I'm not allowed to speak it, if my dad's not allowed to speak it, then bitch you definitely are not supposed to be speaking it. Especially in this context.

I see.

A microaggression is supposedly a window into the psyche of aggressors in which caldrons of racism and offense simmer, waiting for their chance to erupt out of the mouth. On campuses across America, that's a given.

Accepted as proven fact is the assertion that bigotry has been driven underground, but still is alive and kicking in non-marginalized (that is to say, cisgender, white male) society. More than a theory, it is presented as a scientifically proven pathology that blossoms out of the very nature of whiteness, maleness, and every other privileged person. Is it a gene? Or is the white power structure so ingrained into American society that whiteness is learned behavior, not unlike a Southern accent? Whatever the cause, racism and all the other isms are ubiquitous, requiring deep excavation to tear up their roots.

Inconveniently for the microaggression activists, the science does not back up such claims.

In this regard, quoting Scott O. Lilienfeld, the Samuel Candler Dobbs Professor of Psychology at Emory University, at length in Sage Journals' *Perspectives on Psychological Science* is advisable. In "Microaggressions: Strong Claims, Inadequate Evidence," Lilienfeld argues:

The microaggression concept has recently galvanized public discussion and spread to numerous college campuses and businesses. I argue that the micro-aggression research program (MRP) rests on five core premises, namely, that microaggressions (1) are operationalized with sufficient clarity and consensus to afford rigorous scientific investigation; (2) are interpreted negatively by most or all minority group members; (3) reflect implicitly prejudicial and implicitly aggressive motives; (4) can be validly assessed using only respondents' subjective reports; and (5) exert an adverse impact on recipients' mental health.

A review of the literature reveals negligible support for all five suppositions. More broadly, the MRP has been marked by an absence of connectivity to key domains of psychological science, including psychometrics, social cognition, cognitive-behavioral therapy, behavior genetics, and personality, health, and industrial-organizational psychology. Although the MRP has been fruitful in drawing the field's attention to subtle forms of prejudice, it is far too underdeveloped on the conceptual and methodological fronts to warrant real-world application. I conclude with 18 suggestions for advancing the scientific status of the MRP, *recommend abandonment of the term "microaggression," and call for a moratorium on microaggression training programs and publicly distributed microaggression lists pending research to address the MRP's scientific limitations.* [Emphasis added.]

In other words, everyone's jumping the gun, as faculty, students and administrators feverishly try to impose an authorized script on anyone wanting to think and speak for himself.

A raft of scholars and psychologists also expose the dangers of the current obsession with microaggression. Among them is the distinguished sociologist Amitai Etzioni, who wrote, "In short, the movement to overcome micro-aggressions is part naïve idealism, part slightly disguised anti-elite rhetoric, part theater of the absurd. Above all, it draws energy to micro issues in a world full of macro ones," citing ISIS brutalities, police shooting black men, gang warfare that has turned cities into war zones, and the U.S. Supreme Court's *Citizens United* decision that ruled that "bribery is a form of free speech."

Well, I have to disagree with the professor about some of the "bigger issues," but the point he's making is valid. All that time spent on microaggressions is drawing us away from the bigger issues, whether they are issues of the left or right.

Etzioni mentioned a few other problems. A person accused of using microaggressions has no defense, because in his privileged ivy tower he's ignorant of his hidden bias. Only an "offended" person can determine if it's a microaggression. The victim is the prosecutor, judge, and jury all in one. There's no appeal. And the use of "check your privilege" means that anything you might hazard saying is tainted by your unearned advantages. "It basically implies that white males should mince their words, listen rather than talk."

So, if you're at a loss to know what to say, many colleges have formal speech codes that'll set you straight.

8

Thou Shalt Not Embarrass

When it comes to college speech codes, apparently *Ignorantia juris non excusat*, or "ignorance of the law is no excuse" applies. It doesn't matter if you didn't know that the word or expression that you used offended someone. Nor does it matter that it isn't even listed in your school's forbidden, hurtful words inventory. Tough. Off you go to the House of Corrections.

What this brings to mind is the famous 1993 case of a white University of Pennsylvania freshman, Eden Jacobowitz, who got busted for calling four black women students "water buffalo." He had leaned out his dormitory window and yelled at the women outside because they were making a ruckus that was interrupting his studying: "Shut up, you water buffalo. If you're looking for a party, there's a zoo a mile from here.'" The women charged with him "racial harassment" and his academic world came crashing down.

Jacobowitz denied that his comment had anything to do with race. He said it roughly translated from the Hebrew word for "foolish person." Never mind that "water buffalo" wasn't forbidden in the school's speech code and no one could figure out why "water buffalo" was supposed to be racist. The school went ahead and charged him anyway with violating the university's hate speech provisions of the Code of Conduct, and proceeded to find him guilty. The school graciously said it wouldn't put a black mark on his record if he issued an apology, attended a racial sensitivity seminar, and went on dormitory probation.

Jacobowitz refused—good going, Eden. Instead, he filed a fifty-thousand-dollar lawsuit. It took three years, but the university finally settled for less than ten thousand dollars, of which Jacobowitz got nothing. It went for his lawyer's expenses. The school admitted to no wrongdoing. I guess the school figures it has improved its educational climate by successfully exorcising "water buffalo" from the student body lingo.

In other words, even vaguely or ludicrously defined "hate" speech gets no First Amendment protections on some college campuses. Never mind that the U.S. Supreme Court has a different view.

To continue with ludicrous examples, here's one for the books: You must not let the name Harambe pass your lips. Making the *National Review*'s "16 Most Ridiculously PC Moments on College Campuses in 2016" was the University of Massachusetts, where it was decreed that any "negative remarks regarding 'Harambe'" were "direct attack[s] to our campus's African American community" and that certain Harambe jokes were "sexual assault incidences." And, a similar ban was promulgated at Clemson University because of concerns about "racism" and "rape culture." And, a Florida State University poster warned students that Harambe Halloween costumes were "cultural appropriation." The magazine noted that "Harambe is not a culture; he was a gorilla at the Cincinnati Zoo."

Huh? So, what is (a) Harambe? The reference was to a gorilla named Harambe that apparently tried to rescue a three-year-old boy who fell into his pit, but zoo officials, fearing for the child's life, shot the gorilla to death. Okay, so how did Harambe violate the speech codes?

Certainly not from the sympathetic memes showing up on the internet, proclaiming, "Harambe is love," "Harambe is life," "Harambe for President 2016," and "Harambe is a gorilla god." The trouble seemingly erupted from posts that said, "Dicks out for Harambe." It was an odd way of expressing praise, first created by a college student to celebrate him as a symbol of resistance against bad stuff. From there, all kinds of meanings flooded the internet, from it's a statement for closeted gays to show their genitalia to each other without seeming gay to a vicious attack on African Americans. Some interpreted it to mean "guns out" as a symbol for revenge for the gorilla's death. Others concluded that the act of pulling out your penis was a "sign of respect for our fallen hero, Harambe." Others blamed the alt-right for turning it into a racial insult. Not a moment was lost before the hate speech constabulary nailed down these various meanings as clearly racially offensive. Even before they became known as racially offensive. Granted that some of those meanings can be offensive, but the First Amendment protects all the meanings, good or bad.

The examples of speech codes going off the rails are too numerous to itemize here. What follows are just a few:

A University of Michigan psychology grad student whose specialty was in the field of biopsychology—the interdisciplinary study of the biological bases of individual differences in personality traits and mental abilities—was worried that the controversial field would be perceived as "sexist" and "racist" by some students. And that the speech code would stifle legitimate classroom discussion.

According to federal court filings in the landmark *Doe v. University of Michigan*, the student said he feared "that discussion of such theories might be sanctionable under the [school's speech code]. He asserted that his right to freely and openly discuss these theories was impermissibly chilled, and he requested that the policy be declared unconstitutional and enjoined on the grounds of vagueness and overbreadth." Indeed, the court found that students had been disciplined or threatened with discipline for "offensive" remarks made in a classroom setting. "At least one student was subject to a formal hearing because he stated in the context of a social work research class that he believed that homosexuality was a disease that could be psychologically treated," the court said. The grad student's fears of "prosecution were entirely reasonable," the court held. Coming down on the student's side, the court ruled that the policy was too far-reaching and overly broad.

Undoubtedly, universities are trying to find a balance between free speech on one hand and ending racial incidents and protecting the university's educational climate on the other hand. But the federal district court in the above case cited a U.S. Supreme Court decision that proclaimed, "If there is any star fixed in our constitutional constellation, it is that no official, high or petty, can prescribe what shall be orthodox in politics, nationalism, religion, or other matters of opinion or force citizens to confess by word or act their faith therein." Or as in another high court case: "It is firmly settled that under our Constitution the public expression of ideas may not be prohibited merely because the ideas are themselves offensive to some of their hearers." And it further quoted historian and free speech expert C. Vann Woodward, who said, "Freedom of expression is a paramount value, more important than civility or rationality." Woodward later observed, "It simply seems unnatural to make a fuss about the rights of a speaker who offends the moral or political convictions passionately held by a majority. The far more natural impulse is to stop the nonsense, shut it up, punish it—anything but defend it. But to give rein to that inclination would be to make the majority the arbiters of truth for all. Furthermore, it would put the universities into the business of censorship."

You'd think that was clear enough, but schools, under pressure from liberal groups and lawmakers, keep overstepping.

Socialism has come to America. We must defeat it Professors glamorize a system they never lived under, they spread lies about Marxism to college students who aren't told the truth about freedom!

—@charliekirk11, Jan. 22, 2018

Kentucky State University listed, among punishable offenses against persons, "physical assault," "coercion," "threats," and "embarrassment." Embarrassment? As Jonathan Marks remarked in *Commentary* magazine about the sin of causing embarrassment, "I suppose, in theory, it directly affects [anyone's] ability to point out the schmutz on a classmate's shirt."

Harvey Silverglate is a Cambridge, Massachusetts attorney, a veteran defender of civil rights and civil liberties, and co-founder, along with University of Pennsylvania professor Alan Charles Kors, of the Foundation for Individual Rights in Education (FIRE). In a speech accepting the Manhattan Institute's Alexander Hamilton Award, he said of college speech codes:

> Regardless of the justification, definitions of "harassment" were adopted that were so vague and broad so as to escalate the numbers of disciplinary proceedings, many of which were deemed confidential so that the outside world had no idea what was happening. Speech codes popped up that sought to prevent students from insulting or offending one another, but in practice the codes strangled the academic enterprise. Kangaroo courts were established to adjudicate the many violations of the new rules. Remember that we're talking about liberal arts colleges, not prisons, not re-education camps!

He tells a story of how he was hired by some faculty members at the University of Wisconsin to fight a speech code adopted by student life bureaucrats designed to prevent offensive expression: "I didn't actually win that battle. You know who won it? A gay student got up and said, 'If you're looking to have a speech code to protect me, don't do it, because I actually like knowing who hates me. It's useful. It tells me when I should watch my back.'"

FIRE is now a preeminent defender of campus speech. In a recent report, it said:

> Despite the critical importance of free speech on campus, too many universities—in policy and in practice—chill, censor, and punish students' and faculty members' expressive activity. One way that universities do this is through the use of speech codes: policies prohibiting speech that, outside the bounds of campus, would be protected by the First Amendment.

Encouragingly, however, it observed that in the face of court decisions, and I should add common sense, the number of campus speech codes is declining.

> FIRE surveyed 461 colleges and universities for this report and found that just under one-third (32.3 percent) of those schools maintain severely restrictive, "red light" speech codes that clearly and substantially prohibit constitutionally protected speech. While even one speech code is too many, this year [2017] is the tenth year in a row that the percentage of red light schools has declined, and this year's drop was more than seven percentage points. (Last year, 39.6 percent of schools earned a red light rating.)

If you're a student and wonder where all of this leaves you, pay attention to FIRE's advice: "That the First Amendment applies on the public university campus is settled law. Public universities have long occupied a special niche in the Supreme Court's First Amendment jurisprudence. Indeed, the Court has held that First Amendment protections on campus are necessary for the preservation of our democracy."

Listen to those words: "necessary for the preservation of our democracy." The suppression of free speech by the left in academia is antithetical to America's form of government. Allowed to continue as it has puts America in serious jeopardy of bending in subservience of a dictatorial government. That goes for any government of whatever persuasion. It should be emphasized that the work being done by FIRE, Turning Point, and the other conservative defenders of free speech protects expressions from the left as well as the right. Would that the left would be as committed to our freedoms.

So, speak your mind.

9

Free Speech Is Spoken Over There Only

Among the more puzzling leftist fads on campus has been free speech zones. Under the guise of encouraging and protecting free speech, some colleges designated tiny areas on campus for free speech, meaning—what?—that the rest of the campus is a shut-your-mouth, go-away zone?

Flying in the face of the traditional idea that the entire campus is a free speech zone, the zone's teenie-tiny foot-print sometimes is smaller than a Pickle Ball court. You've got to wait your turn to squeeze into the zone because, of course, you must register with the school administration and clear all the requirements. Only then can you be *authorized* to speak your mind, hand out literature, set up a recruiting table, assemble with your signs for a protest, or, ironically, call for the end of those restrictive free speech zones.

Thus, for example, conservative activists have been banned from handing out copies of the U.S. Constitution except in some out-of-sight, out-of-earshot hinterland. Tender ears and eyes are thus protected from unauthorized literature that explains how our system of government works and protects our rights. Ostensibly, free speech zones are meant to protect protestors (from what isn't clear) while preserving the "educational environment." The zones appeared during the Civil Rights and anti-war movements of the '60s and '70s when some protests got out of hand, such as the 1968 Democratic Convention riots in Chicago. But attempts to restrict protestors at the convention backfired as they broke out of designated areas and angrily flooded downtown, prompting what then was called a "police riot" in retaliation. The Kent State University fatal shooting of four student anti-war protestors also was cited as a demonstrable need to bring order to what some saw as the out-of-control abuse of the rights of free speech and assembly.

How these violent events affected the thinking of so many colleges in light of the seemingly mild protests in the twenty-first century might be blamed on overly cautious administrators who lived through that era. But that's hardly an excuse for this reactionary behavior. Outrageously, in the name of promoting free speech, colleges are actually muzzling it. For some schools, there's obviously just too much free speech going on.

In 2013, the Foundation for Individual Rights in Education (FIRE) discovered that one in six of America's four hundred top colleges have such zones. Seventy zones unconstitutionally infringed on free speech and assembly. The

University of Cincinnati's former free speech zone comprised just 0.1 percent of the campus. At many schools, students had to wait five-to-ten business days to get access.

One example: On Constitution Day, three Modesto Junior College students had been handing out copies of the U.S. Constitution in front of the student center for about ten minutes when a campus police officer showed up to stop them. When one student, Robert Van Tuinen, pointed out that they were exercising a constitutional right, the officer sent them into the bureaucratic abyss—the Student Development Office. There, a clerk officiously pulled out the school's "time, place and manner policy" that required students to register five days in advance for any events, all of which were confined in a small free speech corral. And because someone was using the zone then, it could be days, even weeks, before the zone would be available.

When the school administration refused to change the policy, FIRE, working with Van Tuinen and the law firm of Davis Wright Tremaine, filed a federal law suit that led to a settlement that allowed free expression in the open areas of the campus and paid Van Tuinen fifty thousand dollars.

Here's another, more recent example from FIRE: Kevin Shaw, a student at Los Angeles Pierce College, worked with FIRE to sue the school after he was barred from handing out Spanish-language copies of the Constitution on behalf of Young Americans for Liberty. He was outside of the free speech pen that was about the size of three parking spaces, or .003 percent of the campus. The court ruled that open, outdoor areas of Pierce's campus are public forums for student speech, regardless of what the school wants to call them.

The courts, thankfully, have not been kind to the idea of quarantining free speech. For example, Texas Tech University had limited student speech to one "free speech gazebo." A law school student wanted to use a different area to pass out literature expressing his religious and political views that "homosexuality is a sinful, immoral, and unhealthy lifestyle." But the school turned him down because the "request is the expression of a personal belief and thus is something more appropriate for the free speech area which is the Gazebo area..." In response, the school created additional zones, but still required permission to use them. A federal district court in *Roberts v. Haragan* junked the permission requirement for expressive activities outside the zone, noting that the rule was an unconstitutionally broad restriction on expressive speech with no overriding interest that required the school to restrict speech.

While we are focusing on the suppression of conservative speech, the policies affect all points of view. At Turning Point USA, we believe that free speech should apply to everyone, left or right, as the courts have ruled. But Robert O'Neil, a First Amendment scholar, has observed that free speech zone policies, "while seemingly content-neutral, when you look deeper some of the policies seem to mask content discrimination." No surprise there.

How odd is it that the very institution that historically has been the champion of free speech should be the most enamored with the idea of confining speech to prescribed holding pens. Thanks to the courts' pushback, the number of free speech zones on American campuses appears to be declining. Some state legislators, also fed up with this nonsense, are acting to restrict their use in public universities. Now, only an estimated one in ten schools has them.

But before we get too encouraged, let's take a look at the drivel currently soiling many course catalogs.

10

The Illiberal Arts (and Sciences)

What used to be called a "liberals arts" college education consisted of a wide-ranging core curriculum of basic studies designed to introduce students to the best thinking of scientists, philosophers, theologians, writers, and more to establish a springboard for a lifetime of intellectual stimulation, a broad understanding of the arts and sciences, and individual fulfillment. Generally, the course work featured the Classics, emphasizing, but not limited to, Western thought.

No more. The Classics, which have survived for centuries because of their enduring relevance, have been pushed aside by the proposition that they are little more than the narrow-minded, racist, misogynist, homophobic ramblings of old white men. A smug liberal elite has trashed them, arrogantly presuming to know better and smart enough to create an entirely new explanation of everything. Often with silly results.

The number of pointless, faddish, useless, or unscholarly courses has increased exponentially since 1960s counter-culture-like grand poobahs have overrun college faculties and government grant agencies. You need not turn over too many stones to find courses that explore the inside and outside, top and bottom of victimhood. Entire sociology and political science course offerings have succumbed to the goal of churning out legions of self-absorbed "victims" who have been instructed how they can benefit from the claims that, in new, imaginative, and fanciful ways, they have been marginalized. Just what America needs: a wave of college graduates who see an America infected with malice, animus, and hostility everywhere. It is identity politics gone berserk.

> *The reason why @benshapiro has the number 1 most downloaded podcast, & why @DennisPrager's @prageru is getting 1 billion views a year, and why @jordanbpeterson has millions of followers worldwide is our college students are starving for wisdom.*
>
> —*@charliekirk11, Jan. 20, 2018*

Sub-specialties pop up like mushrooms on a damp forest floor advising the put-upon about such things as "intersectionality"—how patterns of discrimination against "marginalized" persons and groups meet or overlap to elevate victimhood to more than the sum of its parts. English lit courses zero in on previously hidden and perverse examples of misogyny in unexpected places and laud new masterpieces of the bizarre, such as *The Handmaid's Tale*.

Gender studies reshape male and female into unrecognizable and preposterous forms. In a race not to be left behind, schools are creating whacky gender, sexuality, and feminist studies departments that feast on government grants, as well as grants from foundations run by progressives, student tuition, and alumni donations. History departments, for example, examine the fluidity of gender roles in medieval society.

One doesn't have to study gender to encounter the latest progressive cant. At Williams College, you can be indoctrinated into "Racial Capitalism" that "will interrogate the ways in which capitalist economies have 'always and everywhere' relied upon forms of racist domination and exclusion." Theology courses have morphed into examinations of Queer God.

"The Unbearable Whiteness Of Barbie" was mandatory for some freshmen at Occidental College. Its description opens new pathways into understanding that "scientific racism has been put to use in the making of Barbie."

Also at Occidental (what's going on there anyway?) was a course that examined the "signification of the phallus" and the "relation of the phallus to masculinity, femininity, genital organs and the fetish." It's an important part of the college's Intercultural and Queer program.

"Politicizing Beyoncé," taught in the Women and Gender Studies Department at the State University of New Jersey, examines the star "as a progressive, feminist, and even queer figure...alongside readings on the history of black feminist struggle in the U.S." to answer the pressing question: "Can Beyoncé's music be seen as a blueprint for progressive social change?" Not to be outdone, Mount Holyoke College's "Whiteness: The Other Side of Racism" indoctrinates students about their role as white members of society.

Harvard's sociology department has raised post-traumatic stress syndrome from an individual affliction to a society-wide suffering in its course, "Social Trauma and Collective Identity." The explanation: "Even though trauma is often a personal experience, it can also affect groups, regions, and even whole nations. This course explores the notion of social trauma by focusing on its emergence, commemoration, and transmission in different societies. How do ideas of trauma stay constant across generations? And what are the consequences of these processes in a variety of sites such as politics, social activism, art, and domestic life?"

Beats me. But it does create an image of an entire country losing it, as depicted in *The Scream*, the painting by Norwegian Expressionist artist Edvard Munch.

There's more, much more: A never-ending and constantly regenerating supply, really. For example: Making the Daily Caller's catalog of "The DUMBEST College Courses For 2015" are: "On Being Bored" (Brown), "Wasting Time On The Internet" (University of Pennsylvania), "How to Win a Beauty Pageant: Race, Gender, Culture, and U.S. National Identity" (Oberlin College), "Tree Climbing" (Cornell), "Stupidity" (Occidental College), "Tattoos, Piercing, and Body Adornment" (Pitzer College), "Women, Culture, and Society: Pop Culture Politics" (Rutgers), "Kanye Versus Everbody! [sic]" (Georgia State), "The American Vacation" (U. of Iowa), "The Sociology of Miley Cyrus: Race, Class, Gender, and Media" (Skidmore), and "Demystifying the Hipster" (Tufts). Finally, the University of California, San Francisco, offers an online course, "Abortion: Quality Care and Public Health Implications." Among its features are weekly lectures that "will incorporate the stories of women who seek abortion in order to better portray abortion significance and rationale." Noticeably absent are women who suffered from an abortion—as if there were no bad side effects. Also absent, the deadly impact of abortion on voiceless unborn babies.

One can safely assume that many of these courses are taught by the likes of Sara Goldrick-Rab, a sociology professor at the University of Wisconsin-Madison, who tweeted how Wisconsin Governor Scott Walker strongly resembles Adolf Hitler. Walker, don't you know, advocated repealing state teacher tenure guarantees and cutting higher-education spending, clearly symptoms of a genocidal mind.

Or teachers who concoct government "studies" like "Constructing masculinized sportscapes: Skiing, gender and nature in British Columbia, Canada," by Memorial University of Newfoundland associate professor Mark C. J. Stoddart. In laymen's terms, ski slopes are sexist. According to Stoddart, ski slopes are "for performing athletic, risk-seeking masculinity," and "less risky areas of the skiing landscape may be interpreted as 'gender-neutral' or feminized space." I won't bother you with the rest.

Just one more, if you can stand it: "The gender politics of glaciers," funded by, of all things, the National Science Foundation (i.e., taxpayers). In it, Mark Carey of the University of Oregon and his fellow researchers outline "A *feminist glaciology framework* for global environmental change research." [Emphasis added.] Say they in the paper's abstract:

> Glaciers are key icons of climate change and global environmental change. However, the relationships among

gender, science, and glaciers—particularly related to epistemological questions about the production of glaciological knowledge—remain understudied. This paper thus proposes a feminist glaciology framework with four key components: (1) knowledge producers; (2) gendered science and knowledge; (3) systems of scientific domination; and (4) alternative representations of glaciers. Merging feminist postcolonial science studies and feminist political ecology, the feminist glaciology framework generates robust analysis of gender, power, and epistemologies in dynamic social-ecological systems, thereby leading to more just and equitable science and human-ice interactions.

Deeper in the study, we're told:

The root of this paradigm comes from the era of Victorian Imperialism in which manly vigor and scientific discovery provided the dominant way of both understanding and dominating foreign spaces. This results in a total lack of consideration of alternative ways of understanding glacial ice, which is especially troubling in the current age of rapid melt.

If you successfully waded through that gobbledygook, more power to you. I couldn't. If students can honestly justify to their parents, many of whom have borrowed against their homes to send their children to college, why taking such courses is essential to their careers, I would be amazed.

I'm confident the Classics and other scholarship untainted by loopy, progressive brain tics will survive, just as they have for centuries. I believe this to be so because the current fad, just like everything from bell-bottoms to selfie sticks, will be overcome by new ones. And the Classics will always be there to provide wisdom and truth.

11

Warning! Triggers Ahead

We're all acquainted with trigger warnings outside of the college classroom. "Not suitable for young children" on television. Movies rated for their violence. "The following contains graphic images that some might find disturbing" on news shows. But hard-left ideology has turned the concept of warnings into a farce.

Trigger warnings as a system for alerting readers, viewers, or listeners of material they might find difficult or inappropriate got started years ago as a legitimate tool to spare soldiers returning from war suffering from post-traumatic stress disorder, for example. For the soldier, a violent scene in a movie could set off an emotionally crippling response. Same for a rape victim who unexpectedly encounters a passage in a book that triggers her own devastating memories. "Trauma-informed care" is the latest psychological lingo for the procedure.

Well and good. But the need for trigger warnings has been hijacked by today's victimhood culture. In college classrooms, trigger warnings have been stretched beyond recognition. Instructors are encouraged or, worse, directed to issue trigger warnings for every slight, embarrassment, or discomfort that any student might encounter in upcoming material. It's become an integral part of what now is being called "inclusive teaching." No anxious moments of any kind allowed.

Sure, it's common sense for a teacher voluntarily to warn veterans, rape victims, and others suffering from PTSD that they might be in for a rough ride. But the reach of required trigger warnings has become so long on some campuses that it approaches the ridiculous. The need to soothe emotions and lift moods challenges vigorous and rigorous learning. A trigger warning might be required in a sociology class, for example, if discussion turns to a subject like class stratification, and the teacher fears, but doesn't know, if it will hurt the feelings of someone who does not enjoy "white privilege."

For an extraordinary example of the victimhood culture, we turn to Kyriarchy and Privilege, a blog dedicated to shining the spotlight on what it considers to be the most extreme and damaging victimhood. It has managed to combine multi-victimhoods into one massive degradation. (Kyriarchy is from the Greek "lord" or "master" and "to rule or dominate.") According to the website's own definition, Kyriarchy (yes, it's always capitalized) has a mission to "redefine the analytic category of patriarchy in terms of multiplicative intersecting structures of domination.... Kyriarchy is best theorized as a complex pyramidal system of

intersecting multiplicative social structures of superordina-
tion and subordination, of ruling and oppression."

Whatever.

You can get a better idea of what this blather is about
from examining the list of classroom triggers. Here's a
warning about the discussion of any "-ism."

Discussions of -isms, shaming, or hatred of any kind
(racism, classism, hatred of cultures/ethnicities that differ
from your own, sexism, hatred of sexualities or genders that
differ from your own, anti-multiple, non-vanilla shaming,
sex positive shaming, fat shaming/body image shaming,
neuroatypical shaming)...

Oops, they left out "ableism." How could they? Here
are some other warning-worthy items: Eating disorders and
other self-injurious behavior; talk of drug use that is legal,
illegal, or psychiatric; descriptions or pictures of medical
procedures even if they don't contain blood or gore; needles;
corpse, skulls, or skeletons; "Trans* degendering, or anti-
trans* views of bodies"; swearing; insects and snakes; vomit;
pregnancy and childbirth; scarification; Nazi paraphernalia
and—honest—"slimy things."

Oh, yes, there's trypophobia. I had to look it up. It's a fear
of irregular patterns or clusters of small holes like honey-
combs or bubbles. It's not officially recognized as a mental
disorder, at least not yet. Symptoms range from making your
skin crawl to panic attacks. There's not a lot of research about
it, but some scientists suspect that it's the result of biological
revulsion. It's one of those explanations that ends with the
cliché, "More research is needed."

Some questions: How does a teacher know that some-where in his class sits a trypophobe? The teacher has to ask, I suppose. But does he start every semester asking everyone in his class if they require a trigger warning for something from an infinitely long list of possible phobias, insults and discomforts? I can hear it now: "Is there anyone in this class-room suffering from obsessive-compulsive disorder? How about trypophobia? Anyone fear a discussion of slurs, such as 'stupid' or 'dumb'?" The list of possible triggers could go on forever.

To be fair, Kyriarchy and Privilege also lists some serious conditions, such as rape, violence, warfare, and suicide. But I wonder why anyone would sign up for a history class when the mention of war brings on trauma. Or an anatomy class if a discussion of blood throws one into a panic. Or a psychology course when sexual behavior, even consensual (another trigger), is up for study.

What I'm saying is that plenty of practical objections stand in the way of requiring or expecting trigger warnings. Just coming up with every possible trigger warning is not unlike trying to count the grains of sand on South Beach. Do you issue warnings only on the first day of class or every day? Do you have to know that someone is actually in the class who merits a trigger warning or is just the possibility of the presence of a victim enough to require a warning? How do you actually phrase a warning? (A trigger warning, if not done properly, by itself could trigger a bad reaction.) Do you issue a general warning such as, "We'll be talking about rape today"? Or do you go into specifics, such as "Today we're studying in detail the various kinds of physical and

emotional damage that rape does"? Is the discussion of abortion too much for women who have had them? What if a
teacher fails to give a trigger warning and a student files a
complaint that the subject matter made her uneasy? Is the
teacher punished and how?

What of the students? How should they react to a trigger
warning? Get up and leave the class, suffering embarrassment? Or can a student insist that something shouldn't be
discussed because a trigger warning alerted her to offensive
material? Can material needing a trigger warning be included
on an exam, making a student who was triggered responsible for knowing and studying the material? Or should the
student be exempted from knowing the material and thus fail
to meet the full prerequisite for receiving credit for having
taken the course?

Should students be required to provide trigger warnings
during classroom discussions? Should students outside of the
classroom—dorms, fraternities, sororities, at work, and even
at parties—give trigger warnings during conversations with
other students?

This is suffocating.

I could go on. But there are even better reasons for being
extraordinarily cautious about demanding trigger warnings.
The University of Chicago expressed it so well in its intro-
ductory letter to incoming freshmen when it warned that
the school does not support trigger warnings. After the letter
became public and the backlash began, university President
Robert J. Zimmer eloquently defended it in a *Wall Street
Journal* op-ed.

He bluntly declared that "free speech is at risk" in academe. He said:

> "Universities cannot be viewed as a sanctuary for comfort but rather as a crucible for confronting ideas and thereby learning to make informed judgments in complex environments. Having one's assumptions challenged and experiencing the discomfort that sometimes accompanies this process are intrinsic parts of an excellent education. Only then will students develop the skills necessary to build their own futures and contribute to society."

While some schools, such as Purdue University, have adopted the same policy, the University of Chicago took heat, not unexpectedly, reported the *New York Times*. Some came from within higher education establishment, with critics calling the concern about trigger warnings "overblown." Michael S. Roth, president of Wesleyan University, called the letter a "PR stunt." History Professor Kevin Gannon at Grand View University in Des Moines said the letter was "a manifesto looking for an audience." Even some of University of Chicago's own students disagreed with the letter, incorrectly insisting that "hate speech," as defined by them, is not constitutionally protected. The same can be heard across the country as students and supporting faculty contend that the campus is, first of all, a "home" where people's feelings should not be hurt. No wonder polls show that a majority of college students believe that they cannot speak their minds without running into a buzz saw of criticism.

On the other side of Chicago, the philosophy of the school as a safe space has taken hold of DePaul University. As a private (Catholic) university, First Amendment speech protections don't apply as they do at a public university. The DePaul example demonstrates how an anti-academic atmosphere can grip a private school when the shut-your-mouth attitude grips the administration, faculty and students.

At DePaul, some students, engaging in a not-unusual form of expression, had chalked some pro-Trump messages on campus sidewalks. Just the name of Trump seemingly offended some and the school's grounds crew soon showed up to erase the messages. Vice President of Student Affairs Eugene Zdziarski then closed down partisan chalking with the made-up excuse that, as a tax-exempt entity, DePaul can't get involved in political campaigns. It's bunk because, as FIRE explained, tax-exempt institutions can't endorse candidates, but students can. It pointed out: "And, as precedent from the Supreme Court of the United States as well as relevant Internal Revenue Service materials make clear, students are presumed to speak for themselves and not for their university." In effect, the school's policy said that no eyes should fall on an "offensive" message, even though the world is full of them. Because this is a chapter about trigger warnings, I'm wondering if the pro-Trump chalking would have been okay if a sign had been posted alongside the sidewalk with something like, "Proceed with Caution, traumatic pro-Trump chalking ahead." I guess not, because just the sight of anything outside their convictions would send students fleeing to a safe place, for cookies, hot chocolate, and cuddly squeeze toys.

While solid figures are not readily available on the extent to which trigger warnings are used or required, National Public Radio conducted a non-scientific survey in 2016 of 829 teachers, of which almost 65 percent of respondents said they issued trigger warnings. The respondents said they generally provide trigger warnings for sexual or violent material, and to a lesser degree for racially, religiously, or politically charged material. Fewer than two percent said their schools had official policies about their use. But, as we see, that can be deceptive.

Defenders of trigger warnings would have us believe that they're no big deal because they're voluntary and that no schools make them mandatory. Samantha Harris challenges that assertion on FIRE's blog. In "Think Trigger Warnings Are Never Mandatory on Campus? Think again," she notes that Drexel University's Sexual and Gender-Based Harassment and Misconduct Policy states: "[i]t is expected that instructors will offer appropriate warning and accommodation regarding the introduction of explicit and triggering materials used." She notes that four other colleges use the same exact language and who knows how many more colleges use different language to accomplish the same purpose. The problem is that the directives, admonitions, or mandates—call them whatever you want—about trigger warnings might be so vague that a teacher could be punished for anything that even remotely suggests that the teacher was being insensitive to the needs of any student who files a formal complaint.

Harris noted that Title IX, the federal law banning sexual discrimination in schools, can be so broadly applied that it could be interpreted to require the warnings and punish teachers or schools that don't provide them. It's hard to argue with that after the Obama administration's Department of Education used Title IX to force an Illinois high school to allow a student, born male but self-identifying as female, to shower and change with girls in the locker room. Harris cited a case at the University of Denver where the school upheld a sexual harassment claim under Title IX against a professor who, in his graduate course on the drug war, included a section on "Drugs and Sin in American Life: From Masturbation and Prostitution to Alcohol and Drugs."

Other trigger warning enthusiasts argue that their negative effects are over-stated, insisting that cautions are not used to "pamper" students. They say they're only used to protect PTSD sufferers from the genuine biological and psychological reactions that can lead to panic—everything from shortness of breath to fainting. But without adequate research, it's also possible to hypothesize that the "need" for trigger warnings is overblown. Where is the research, for example, that proves that forewarnings are needed or that they are effective in preventing multiple PTSD-related incidents, other than discomfort? How many such incidents occur in classrooms in the first place?

Look, I want to be clear: Of course, warnings are appropriate for students who have suffered from combat, sexual abuse, domestic violence, witnessing gang killings, and other trauma that can bring on extreme emotional or physical reactions. Although it strikes me that students are smart enough when they sign up for courses to know, to some degree, what to expect.

More to the point, though, is that trigger warnings are a symptom of the larger problem gripping college campuses: The idea that speech should and can be directed by higher authority in a setting in which discourse, disagreement, and dispute are an essential part of the very definition of the endeavor. And that one side is right while the other side should put aside their arguments in silent consent to the autocratic left.

12

The White Privilege Indoctrination

Nothing like the notion of "white privilege" illustrates how quickly the poison that the left is cooking up on college campuses can contaminate America. Sowed by hard-left racists, the idea blossomed in sociology, political science, history, and other college "disciplines," and now is reseeding itself in mainstream thought. Anyone who dares challenge this racist theory is immediately labeled a racist.

It's a collegiate pandemic. A University of Wisconsin-Madison course explains, "The Problem of Whiteness." A lecture at Dartmouth asks, "What's up with whiteness?" A course at Ohio State examines "Waking up White: What it means to accept your legacy, for better and worse," and "White privilege: unpacking the invisible knapsack." A Sam Houston State course promises to make students aware of their "white racial literacy." A course at Hunter College advocates "The abolition of whiteness"—which would be fighting words if applied to "blackness." Such courses laughably claim they are teaching "tolerance." White privilege, they instruct us, pervades every corner of our society. It goes with skin color; it's not something you choose. It just is.

> *After 5 years of doing campus organizing and speeches, I have learned that most college students are not opposed to conservative ideas, instead they are never properly exposed to them in the first place.*
> —*@charliekirk11, Jan. 22, 2018*

Chicago Tribune columnist Dahleen Glanton aptly demonstrated how these tropes are settling in comfortably into the mainstream media. "If you are a white person in America, you were born privileged," she wrote. "That's just a fact. It's nothing to be ashamed of. It's not anybody's fault. There's no need to get defensive about it. The best thing to do is just acknowledge it."

No need to get defensive? When an entire race is being singled out and stereotyped on the basis of skin color?

And what is it that we're supposed to acknowledge? Frances E. Kendall, a self-described expert on diversity and white privilege, posed this puzzling explanation: Whites, who are "born with access to power and resources," are blinded by their power and resources, especially those white people who don't feel powerful or who don't have power and resources. She goes on: "It is sort of like asking fish to notice water or birds to discuss air. For those who have privileges based on race or gender or class or physical ability or sexual orientation, or age, it just is—it's normal."

In other words, born white, *ipso facto*, privileged.

It's more than a *belief* in racial superiority, such as what white power racists promote. It is an assertion that white people *actually* are born superior, equipped as they are by society and history with more powerful resources. White people must acknowledge that they are more powerful because their skin color makes them more powerful, not for any genetic reason, but because society endows them with power—merely on the basis of their skin color. You need to acknowledge your power, even if you don't have power.

Enough. These arguments circle around and bite themselves on the butt. It's a Catch-22: If you're white you have power, except when you don't have power, but still you must acknowledge having power.

Let's make it simple, the way it should be:

> I have a dream that my four little children will one day
> live in a nation where they will not be judged by the
> color of their skin but by the content of their character.

Those words, spoken by the Reverend Martin Luther King on the steps of Lincoln Memorial during the historic March on Washington, have become as much a part of the American lexicon as "all men are created equal." It was an uncomplicated and true formula that is as relevant today as it was in 1963. It was memorialized by people of good will as the embodiment of America's lofty goals, as yet unattained. School children memorized these stirring words in speeches. These words repeatedly encouraged those who struggled against racism and brought light into America's darkest corners.

Today, the left challenges the clarity of those words, suggesting that they mean something besides what they say. The left has watered down those words to the point of near emptiness. Today, conservatives are the guardians of those words, arguing that they mean exactly what they say. Whatever the state of racial relations today, I dare say a colorblind society, in which the individual is valued for his own intrinsic human worth, is the ultimate American objective.

For leftists, skin color is the *sine qua non*—the most essential consideration—in public policy debate. The left is obsessed with race. The left can't stop talking about race. For the left, you're not so much an individual as you are a subset of a clan. You don't have the capacity to be creative, aspirational, compassionate, just, or fair because racism supposedly is so systemic that escaping the handcuffs of group-think is impossible.

The left has chosen to betray King's legacy and, they themselves, have become racists. They have compartmentalized and segmented people based solely on their skin type. They have delegitimized people. Tragically, in this the left itself refuses to acknowledge the damage they do to people and the danger they pose to our form of government. Not the least of those in danger are the minorities who take it to heart that they cannot escape their oppression until privileged whites admit their sins and release people of color from their bondage.

> *Betsy DeVos was booed & had backs turned at a*
> *Historically Black College She is fighting for school*
> *choice which will help blacks the most!*
>
> —@charliekirk11, May 10, 2017

They keep saying, "white privilege, white privilege." But there are other types of privilege. There is hard work privilege. There is good choice privilege. There is marriage privilege, in which you live longer, have fewer strokes and heart attacks, have a lower chance of becoming depressed, and are more likely to survive cancer longer. You do really well in America when you make good choices.

Sadly, government incentivizes bad choices, particularly in urban areas and in minority communities, particularly in our welfare system or in broken public schools. When people make bad choices for generation after generation, those communities start to deteriorate, crime goes up, and the whole school system falls apart.

We need an infusion of common sense and straight talk when it comes to privilege and oppression. Words such as those spoken by Candace Owens, communications director for Turning Point USA, when protestors from Black Lives Matter objected to her, as a black woman, speaking her own mind about white privilege. To them, this strong black woman replied:

[Your] victim mentality is not cool. I don't know why people like being oppressed. It's the weirdest thing I have ever heard. "I love oppression. We are oppressed. Four hundred years of slavery, Jim Crow." Which, by the way, none of you guys lived through. Your grand-parents did. It's embarrassing you utilize their history. You are not living through anything right now. You are overly privileged Americans.

She later tweeted, "They're a bunch of whiny toddlers, pretending to be oppressed for attention." Support quickly arrived from rap star Kanye West who said, "I love the way Candace Owens thinks." Even quicker, organized sufferers lit up social media heaping condemnations on West for being a black man who dares to deviate from the clichés about white privilege. And they aimed their guns at Owens. "In about 10 seconds [after Kanye's tweet] I became the KKK member, anti-LGBT, you name it. Just because I think differently and I refuse to accept this narrative that I'm a victim. I'm not a victim."

Owens is speaking truth to power—the power that the left wing has aggregated on college campuses and whose pap has spilled over into the media and America in general. Ameri-can universities need a wake-up call, and Owens, West, and a few others are courageous enough to give it. Are the rest of us, especially students who are sick of the racist attacks, willing to join in?

13

Black Victimization Bunco

Candace Owens is changing America's conversation about race. Changing it for the better. Changing it to be more honest. Especially on college campuses, where black victimization is practiced as if it were a post-graduate course of study and taught as if it were holy writ.

Along comes Candace, Turning Point's communications director, to figuratively nail on academe's door her powerful and eloquent challenges of the left's dogma that if you're black, you best stay back. Stay back where skin color defines how you think. Stay back where dependence and entitlement run—ruin, I should say—your life. Stay back where group think are the chains that bind.

Candace is telling students, faculty, and administrators that, in their determination to help the marginalized, they are, in fact, victimizing them. Prominent among them are African Americans who Owens is determined to lead into the promised land of independent thought and action.

"[T]hey [the left] think that they have a monopoly not just on our students, which is what we deal with at Turning Point USA, but also on the entire black race in America," she boldly tells the left. "They have created a mental prison for all of us. And the second somebody runs off what I refer to as the 'Democratic plantation,' they send the dogs out," she said on one of her increasing number of appearances on national media, this with Fox News host Laura Ingraham.

Owens has raised the profile of Turning Point and our message of liberty and free markets. We're proud of the work she has done and thankful for her great successes. The national attention I wrote about in the previous chapter turns the light on the left's excesses, not just on college campuses, but also across America. And overseas, as her popular videos have been dubbed into French and Portuguese.

Her dynamism and honesty inspire all of us personally. I am constantly amazed by her courage and her willingness to plunge head-first into the hate-filled controversies inspired by mindless Hollywood celebrities, self-serving politicians, and partisan media. For me, she energizes my determination to continue fighting for liberty and opens my mind to new and exciting strategies for this all-important battle to save generations from leftist brainwashing.

I want to stand up and cheer when she responds to the bogus charge that she and, by extension those of us at Turning Point, are on the far right, members of the alt-right, and even white supremacists. As she said, "I believe the black community can do it without hand-outs. I believe the Democrats have strapped us to our past to prevent us from our futures.

And I won't stop fighting until all black Americans see that. I'm not far right—I'm free."

Indeed, we are. Free of the left's conformity. To me, she represents the possibility that we are on the threshold of another emancipation: First the end of slavery, then the apartheid-like Jim Crow laws, and now freedom from the left's intellectual and emotional bondage.

Owens wasn't always a conservative. Not until after she had finished college (University of Rhode Island, journalism) and worked several years in a private equity firm, did she see through the fog. She had tried to create an anti-bullying start-up, something she was interested in because she had experienced bullying in school. But as she said, "things went sideways" for the project after she came under attack by progressives who thought her project would unveil anonymous posters, in this case the "trolls" who use the internet to bully people.

The hate mail started rolling in and, under pressure, the online funder Kickstarter cancelled her project. The media picked up on the dispute, exposing her to the liberal bias of reporters who misrepresented her side of the story. She said that made her a conservative overnight. Everything that President Donald Trump was saying about the media was true, she realized. Now she knew first-hand how the media hired hit men.

Upon re-evaluating her views, she now thinks that she always was a conservative. At the end of the day, she always believed in "fact-based, rational, economics." Her first video, a hilarious story of how she broke it to her parents that she was coming out of the closet as a conservative, went viral.

And it revealed a shifting perspective in the black community. She says that she is beginning to see a real split in the black community—those with a victim mentality and those with a victor mentality.

Such bold thinking has catapulted her onto the national stage. The support of rap superstar Kanye West for the way she thinks is only part of her well-deserved fame. She has become a hit on college campuses. She's a ratings star on news shows. Her videos continue to go viral. It's not just the force of her personality and her rhetorical skills. It's what she's saying. Things that the left wants to suppress, not just on college campuses, but everywhere.

For example, she says, from her own experience, that the only thing that's holding blacks back is an obsession with the past. "The biggest problem is that blacks don't know their own history. All they know is what CNN tells them to know. I want to get into the faces of these movements. I want to speak to liberals, to black people."

And what she wants to tell them is a simple, but life-changing message as she, once again, confronts the bogus accusation that she is far right. "Far right? Allow me to clarify," she says. "I believe the black community can do it without hand-outs. I believe the Democrats have strapped us to our past to prevent us from our futures. And I won't stop fighting until all black Americans see that."

She is fighting the "bigotry of low expectations that has been seeded into the consciousness of blacks, sold to us by the extreme left. Over the last decade, blacks have become mentally weak—the weakest we have ever been at any point in our history. Black power has transformed into black submission."

And those who deviate from the victimization fabrications, like Kanye West? "If you are black and think conservative, you're a traitor, an Uncle Tom, a coon. If you're black and someone says to you, 'You must like hip-hop,' that's racist. But if someone says you're black, so you must be a liberal, that's racist too."

As for the Black Lives Matter movement? She has taken them on, she says, "because I believe that their ideas are poisonous. I also believe that they are intellectually dishonest."

The leftist response is always the same: Black people still are struggling to recover from centuries of slavery, Jim Crow, and the privilege that white people have accumulated over the years. Those have created just too many hurdles leading to the false assumption that blacks simply can't do for themselves. They need *the government.*

Her response is swift and accurate. There is an ideological civil war happening: It's between black people who are focused on their past, shouting about slavery, and black people who are focused on their futures. Many of those bewailing the past, who are looking for excuses, who wallow in their victimhood, are certain to fail. For them, an ideology that supports their victimhood is their enemy. The left is their enemy. The blacks who have never been through the torment and struggles of slavery, of lynching, of the denial of the rights of equal employment, voting, open housing, and public accommodations. Those who have never suffered from beatings while marching for those rights, the dehumanizing portrayals in entertainment, and the poverty of share cropping. Of broken promises, of men who fought in wars only to return to a segregated America.

It's worth repeating what she said to them: "It's embarrassing that you utilize their history, you utilize their history and you come in here with more emotion than they ever had when they were living through it. You're not living through anything right now. You're overly privileged Americans."

But not to end on a sour note. Owens also finds that "the most refreshing thing is that here are a lot of people on Facebook who reach out to me and say thank you very much. I can finally come out and say what I think. That I know that I can disagree."

14

The Roots of the Left's Intellectual Chokehold

As weird and laughable as the preceding tour has been of higher education's campaign to indulge emotionally fragile dispositions, what we're witnessing is the dangerous destruction of the healthy skepticism, intellectual curiosity, and passionate search for truth that is the very idea of the university. Worse, more than academe, is in danger. The surrender of the university's carefully constructed and indispensable mission of inquiry throughout history is jeopardizing our cherished form of self-government.

This is not hyperbole. I could not be more serious. The intolerance that is increasingly choking free speech and independent thought on America's campuses is spawning an entire generation whose disrespect for the essential ingredients of democracy is, to put it frankly, horrifying. It is already seeping into the mainstream of American thought and practice.

You'll find it in the articles, editorials and op-ed pages of such doctrinaire newspapers as the *New York Times*, where its hard-left readers tolerate no deviation from the given wisdom as revealed in the college classroom or elsewhere. Op-eds that disagree with the current narrative on, say, "white privilege" have been met with harsh criticism and demands that the writer of such deviant thoughts be purged from the *Times*. Whether the issue is capitalism, illegal immigration, abortion, or any other contentious issues that rock Washington and our state capitals, the die has been cast. Any disagreement reveals an unparalleled level of conservative meanness.

You'll find the same prescriptions written by journalists throughout the country, as terms such as "white privilege" are entering the mainstream. So too are attacks on capitalism and free markets. Polls show that increasing numbers of Millennials are expressing a preference for living under socialism, even though they poorly understand its meaning. For some, socialism is little more than the kind of "sewer socialism" practiced in Milwaukee for the first half of the twentieth century. This brand of socialism meant that the local government owns and operates municipal public utilities such as the electric company, garbage pickup, and public transportation. Conservatives recognize the inefficiencies that are built into government-owned operations. That's unlike self-styled non-socialist progressives who want to governmentalize everything while railing against privatization. Privatization, they argue, is little more than an attack on the public interest by the greedy private sector. Never mind that the rationale for government-run operations time and time again is to provide jobs for patronage workers and contracts for insiders.

You can see how this plays out today in the debate over public education. As it is, "public" education means tuition-free, publicly funded schooling in a public (i.e., government) school system. Strict adherence to this model has resulted in poor performing urban schools, crushing taxation to support the system, and union-control of the budget. Any suggestion that school vouchers, in which public subsidies follow the student instead of being fed into the jaws of government, is considered a betrayal of "the children." Even charter schools run by the private sector, but still under the ultimate control of government, are verboten.

True collectivists, however, go further. They're not just for public control of utilities and schools, but also for "public" control of everything. They adopt the reasoning of Karl Marx, Friedrich Engels, and their admirers. They insist that "the people" should own the "means of production," meaning that government should own factories, transportation, consumer services, and just about everything that would be privately owned and operated. It is a system based on the belief that people cannot be trusted to care for themselves. That they're not smart enough to secure housing, food, and other essentials on their own. That to satisfy their greed, business owners and investors will rip off everyone in sight. That they have no concern for their neighbors or the common good.

It is an extremely dark philosophy. And one that is at war with itself. Consider: If people can't be trusted to care for themselves, then what about a government that is run by... people? If people, left to their own resources, have no sense of the common good or despise their neighbors, then how do they suddenly become enlightened when they go to work for the government?

One can only speculate. Maybe the theory is that only the already enlightened go to work for the government. Or that by going into government, they are smarter and more purely motivated. Or that God or nature has particularly blessed them to be more alert to dangers that the rest of us present to each other. Or that left to on our own, we'll pollute the world and turn the globe into an oven. Walk down the hallway of a Franz Kafka-like bureaucratic honeycomb, open an office door, and you're likely to encounter such an attitude.

How did this philosophy seep into higher education to the point that it is a powerful, if not dominant, force in the classroom? How did liberal and collective absolutism threaten the university's mission of intellectual honesty, if it hasn't overtaken it already?

The liberal response is that conservatives—those of us fighting to preserve higher education's historic mission—are overstating, even exaggerating, the danger because of our ideological blindness or for our own selfish purposes.

Although some studies have challenged the idea that universities have come under the collectivist, socialist or progressive sway, more recent scholarship has moved beyond the "if" and into the "how." Simple observation, as we have done in the forgoing chapters, reveals a campus in the thrall of authoritarian liberal thinking with little appetite for disagreement from the right.

One study suggests that individualists tend to gravitate to non-government opportunities in the private sector because they are more monetarily and personally rewarding than wearing a government straightjacket. I think that these self-motivators don't like government's imposed conformity. They don't like the top-down thinking. True, privately owned companies are not immune to this restrictive culture, but they pale in comparison with the government culture, where regimentation and an authoritarian atmosphere are more commonplace.

But there's more to it than self-selection. Today's absolutist thinking is quite regressive. For most of mankind's history, governments operated in the authoritarian model—Rome with its Caesars, ancient China with its dynasties, Egypt with its pharaohs, Russia with its czars, and a host of European monarchs. Examples of self-government were few and far between. This authoritarian tradition is rooted in a philosophy of handed-down truths, whether sectarian or secular.

In the West, however, thinking had been evolving into a more idiosyncratic mode and finally blossomed in the British colonies in America. Thomas Jefferson eloquently expressed their principles in the Declaration of Independence: "We hold these truths to be self-evident, that all men are created equal, that they are endowed by their Creator with certain unalienable Rights, that among these are Life, Liberty and the pursuit of Happiness." Despite being bad-mouthed today as a slave owner, Jefferson set out the goal that we still are pursuing today.

On the other hand, the idea that "all men" are engaged in an inevitable class war that leads to a utopian society is Marxist-Leninist thinking. Its vision is one of enforced equal results as dictated by higher authority instead of equality of opportunity, one in which each person, by his very nature, is entitled to an identical chance. You can find a straight line of thinking of today's collectivists to the worn-out and demonstrably failed experiments in the Soviet Union, Cuba, Venezuela, and elsewhere. Even places that espouse collectivist governments, such as China and Vietnam, have found success because of their acceptance of capitalist values. Yet, they still fall far short of superior capitalist societies that respect and foster individual initiative.

The divide between collectivists and individualists was aggravated by the 1960s Cultural Revolution. It's still glorified in the media—the Woodstock music festival, the protests against the Vietnam War, agenda feminism, sexual freedom, drugs, the counterculture, communes, the whole bit. While many celebrate the new freedoms that supposedly blessed one and all, a host of other problems were born.

How typical of those times that the young men who burned their draft cards or who fled to Canada to escape the draft were popularly described as courageous heroes, and given a blanket pardon after the war by President Jimmy Carter. No parades were held for returning veterans. More than a decade passed before respect for the military returned.

The '60s far-left, such as the Weather Underground, preached violence as a means to their end. The post-World War Two prosperity of the 1950s created, in the '60s, a generation whose sense of entitlement and self-admiration soured many on the validity of the legitimacy of the American dream. With that came the intolerance and self-satisfied certitude that has blossomed on today's college campuses. Scratch a tenured liberal arts professor today and you are likely to find an admirer of the counter-culture revolution in America or an activist who actually participated in that upheaval. This is where the "flower children" of the '60s have led us.

The '60s outlook has been nurtured and funded by the like-minded. Left-wing ideologues and activists that dominate government funnel hundreds of millions of dollars every year into the social, behavioral, and other soft sciences whose studies "prove" the superiority of left-wing rhetoric. Need evidence that children raised by same-sex parents are just as well adjusted, if not more so, than those raised in a traditional marriage? Voila, here comes a government-funded study to prove it.

Even the hard sciences are not immune. Need evidence of human-caused global warming? Government-funded studies will provide it. Private sector studies that cast doubt on the link between civilization and warming will be mocked as anti-science, merely because they don't have the imprimatur of United Nations-funded bureaucrats and researchers.

Nor should we forget the well-financed foundations that have become handmaids of liberal orthodoxy. On the one hand, liberals enjoy berating the conservative Koch brothers for their humanitarian, educational, and political funding. On the other, they turn to the ultra-liberal billionaire George Soros. Through his Open Society Foundations, Soros reportedly has given more than four hundred million dollars to colleges and universities, while, in comparison, the Koch brothers have contributed a relatively measly seven million dollars. Harvard and Georgetown, bastions of left-wing indoctrination, are among the beneficiaries.

> *The greatest threat to Western civilization is what's going on on our college campuses today.*
> —@charliekirk11, April, 2017

Meanwhile, the Soros foundations donated 7.3 million dollars to his Center for American Progress, to issue a hypocritical report, "Koch Fueling Far Right Academic Centers at Universities across the Country," while Soros' money is fueling larger and wider ranging left wing causes on campus. In 2010, Soros' money funded Columbia University (1.4 million dollars) and Harvard (1.3 million dollars).

Obviously, we don't have a problem with private funding of higher education. Our problem is that if liberals criticize conservative individuals and organizations for contributing to colleges and universities, what are we to make of liberal silence when the far left does the same?

If we are to judge by the results, one might conclude that conservative contributions don't make as much difference as do left-wing contributions. Where we find hope, though, is in the number of students we encounter in our college visits who are determined not to be propagandized and brainwashed. These are the students who turn out for our speeches and debates, who join our Turning Point USA college chapters, and who courageously stand up to intense peer, faculty, and administration pressure from the left.

15

Navigating the Treacherous Terrain

Today's college campus right now is the most treacherous terrain imaginable in America for free speech, independent thinking, academic freedom, and conservative ideas.

Fifty years ago, the University of California at Berkley was the birthplace of the student-led free speech movement. Today, it is a place of intolerance and riots in defense of curbing free speech. Today, the most intolerant people on campus are the ones who preach tolerance. Today, if you're a conservative, you have to sit through four years of indoctrination, yet, according to the leftist mob, you should not be allowed to listen to a guest speaker for even an hour if what he says offends anyone on the left. Today, the left-wing demand for diversity is one based on demographics; there is no room for diversity of opinion.

On college campuses, the classic liberalism of Democrat presidents John F. Kennedy and Lyndon Baines Johnson is moribund, if not already dead. Classic liberalism respected those historic values of free speech as an integral part of the civil rights agenda. While they were considered on the left of the political spectrum, they did not promote the gagging of their opponents' free speech. I am reminded of an older African American professor of that classic liberal era who was told by a student that she was offended by today's lesson. The teacher was puzzled and asked, what do you mean? We talked about the Constitution. The flummoxed professor told National Public Radio she doesn't know what is happening to young liberals today.

So, have we at last come to this: Can we not talk about the bedrock document of our government, with its Bill of Rights and separation of powers, without causing offense? Will that be the next thing the left will demand be exorcised from the curriculum?

As we've seen in example after example throughout this book, today's left cannot tolerate a fair and open forum because they know that when confronted with facts and reason, they lose the debate. So, their strategy is to destroy the discussion and own the narrative. If you want to be the campus rebel, don't be a liberal. If you're a liberal, you'll fit right in with the hard liners who hate the idea that there are other ideas. If you have other ideas, they'll hate you for having them.

The left at first denies that it dominates the faculty, staff, and student body. Confronted with the facts established by studies and anecdotal evidence that they do, they say, so what? If need be, they retreat to the assertion that they've got the truth, so there's no need for discussion. Moreover, they say, those who want to engage in a good, old-fashioned debate are racists, sexists, and a host of other -ists who are evil and on the "wrong side of history." How odd that the left adamantly claims that truth is on their side, but they are disciples of post-modernism, which posits that the notion of objective truth is a fantasy of authoritarian, conservative, backward, and deplorable minds. Tell me; whose minds are closed?

The left's authoritarian tool box is packed with "free speech" codes, "free speech" zones, trigger warnings, micro-aggressions, "safe spaces," "white privilege," and countless other devices that supposedly enable more free speech but, in fact, obstruct and gag free speech.

The left's autocratic training starts on college campuses. It's where journalists get their ideas. It's where reporters and copy editors get indoctrinated. It's where radical 1960s professors land and their clones are birthed. Infiltration of the academe is a deliberate and strategic ploy to move America into a huge-government, collectivist mindset by smashing the historic role of freedom and free-market ideas that have propelled this country to be the most successful in history.

What the left fails to understand is that free speech isn't just saying what you want, but it sometimes means hearing things that make you stop and think. By exposing yourself to things that make you pause and reconsider, you may push your boundaries, and that's a good thing. Having your ideas challenged is as beneficial for your mind as pre-season, summer training camp is for professional football players.

Listening to the other side sharpens your rhetorical skills. It firms up your own beliefs. Or, perhaps, makes you see the error of your ways, ask questions about your own opinions, and moves you to a better, more informed and rational position.

That's why at Turning Point USA, we don't just believe in free speech. We aggressively advocate for it, for liberals as well as for conservatives, and not just because we are a political minority on campus, or because we don't have the ability to silence our opponents. We champion free speech because we feel strongly that it should be a bedrock principle across the political spectrum.

I have no trouble accepting that a socialist has a right to speak; in fact, I welcome the debate, and in all my years of traveling around America's campus, I have not once heard of a conservative individual or group trying to shut down a liberal. That is just not what we do. The same cannot be said of the other side, as over the years they have unleashed well-documented wave after wave of assaults on conservatives.

But what troubles me most about this thuggish behavior is that when we start to selectively edit speech and throw out labels such as hater, bigoted and racist, it shuts down the kinds of discussions that we should be having not just in our institutions of higher learning, but in Congress and our statehouses, and in our personal conversations.

And make no mistake. The welfare of the university is not the only thing at stake here. The damage being perpetrated by left-wing zealots is far more pernicious than that. It's the damage being done to our idea of self-government as the anti-free-market, politically correct blob oozes out from the campus into mainstream thought and action.

> *One of the greatest lies penetrating our universities is the idea we have a country rigged against black people. America is the least racist country in the world. Anyone who comes here can succeed if they make the right choices. White privilege is a racist lie.*
> —@charliekirk11, April 25, 2018

The leftist intolerance machine is extending beyond colleges. Companies such as Amazon use their massive platforms to make negative ratings surrounding Hillary Clinton's book, *What Happened,* disappear. Amazon also has been known for manipulating search results consistently.

Here's how, according to Mashable. Within twenty-four hours of Clinton's book appearing on a Tuesday, Amazon recorded 1,500 reviews, an astonishing number of readers to have waded through a five-hundred-page book in less than a day. Suspecting that partisans were taking over the reviews, Amazon started weeding out the suspects. By mid-day Wednesday, 30 percent of the 707 remaining "verified purchases" were one-star, Amazon's lowest ranking. A day later, of the 620 "verified" reviews, only 3 percent were one-star. Not only did Amazon wipe out the negative reviews, but it overwhelmingly favored the best, five-star reviews. On mid-day Wednesday, Amazon concluded that an impressive 65 percent of the "verified" reviews gave the book the best rating—five stars. But that was nothing; the next day, Amazon concluded that an astonishing 95 percent of the reviewers awarded the book five stars. Only 2 percent gave it a four-star rating and no one gave it a three- or two-star rating. Such laughable results have all the credibility of a Russian or Venezuelan election.

We have also seen Twitter shadow-ban conservative accounts, de-verify important voices such as conservative political activist James O'Keefe, and shut down videos that espouse right-leaning views. The leftist training students are receiving will be with them for a lifetime as they take massively important corporate positions in technology, business, finance, and media.

It's not just the process of shutting down debate that is of such great concern. It's the possibility that collectivism and autocracy, hand in hand, will destroy our republican form of government and our free-market economy. We've seen what has happened in the Soviet Union, Cuba, and tin-pot socialist dictatorships as they plunge into failure, misery, poverty, and violence. That a new generation believes that socialism—as if it was something that it alone has discovered—is the superior form of government, betrays a staggering failure of education today and whatever goofy pedagogy directs the teaching of history.

How laughably ironic, then, that the left doesn't understand the threat *it* poses to democracy while accusing conservatives of creating a "democratic crisis." That's what Hillary Clinton told the Yale University class of 2018: "Right now we're living through a full-fledged crisis in our democracy. No, there are not tanks in the streets, but what's happening right now goes to the heart of who we are as a nation, and I say this not as a Democrat who lost an election but as an American afraid of losing a country."

Al Gore joined in with his warning at the 2018 University of Maryland commencement: "What if, in this year and the years immediately following, something truly extraordinary happened?" He called for "an American youth movement" that would vote in "unprecedented numbers and reclaim the integrity of American democracy."

College graduates nationwide heard this distorted message as liberal commencement speakers in 2018 outnumbered conservatives by a nearly four-to-one margin at the nation's fifty largest colleges, according to Campus Reform. The liberal line-up, in addition to Clinton and Gore, included President Jimmy Carter, Canadian Prime Minister Justin Trudeau, U.S. Representative John Lewis, and U.S. Senators Cory Booker and Kamala Harris. The conservative speakers were lesser lights, usually state officials.

Here's just one example of how the left, itself, is a threat to our form of government. The left asserts that hate speech is not protected under the First Amendment. And they argue that silencing conservatives is justifiable because the conservative agenda is hateful. So, they are astounded when told that the Constitution does, in fact, protect hate speech. As recently as 2017, the U.S. Supreme Court unanimously affirmed that hate speech is not prohibited by the First Amendment.

As Justice Samuel Alito wrote for four justices in *Matal v. Tam*:

[The idea that the government may restrict] speech expressing ideas that offend...strikes at the heart of the

First Amendment. Speech that demeans on the basis of race, ethnicity, gender, religion, age, disability, or any other similar ground is hateful; but the proudest boast of our free speech jurisprudence is that we protect the freedom to express "the thought that we hate."

Justice Anthony Kennedy wrote separately for four justices (Neil Gorsuch wasn't on the court when the case was argued):

A law found to discriminate based on viewpoint is an "egregious form of content discrimination," which is "presumptively unconstitutional."...A law that can be directed against speech found offensive to some portion of the public can be turned against minority and dissenting views to the detriment of all. The First Amendment does not entrust that power to the government's benevolence. Instead, our reliance must be on the substantial safeguards of free and open discussion in a democratic society.

It's just one example of how left-wing mindset poses a danger to our form of government. Here's a better idea of how to deal with hate speech. Have better ideas. The answer to white supremacists and Nazis is not preventing them from showing up on campus. The answer is that you also show up; cross examine them and pump them for honest answers to your challenging questions. If you try to censor them, you're giving them what they want, which is to portray themselves as victims or martyrs. When someone has racist, offensive, or bad ideas, challenge them respectfully. If you are trying to shut them up because you disagree with them, then you are an intellectual midget.

Keep reminding yourself: never try to silence someone. If you're tired of someone being a troll, you can always walk away. You can remove yourself from this conversation. But don't use force to try to stop this conversation. That's when you become a fascist. That's when you land on what I call the campus islands of totalitarianism.

At Turning Point USA, we are not just one of the staunchest defenders of free speech on campus, be we are continually fighting for our other values. Among them: We believe that America is the greatest country in world history; that free enterprise is the most assured way to lift people out of poverty and into prosperity; that the Constitution is the greatest political document ever written by man; that big government needs to be scaled back and reconsidered; and the best solution to our problems is people helping people and entrepreneurs taking risks outside of government intervention. In other words, everything that the left-wing curia has outlawed.

Yet, I believe that today's college-age generation will come to understand and even support the idea of free enterprise and the Constitution when they are explained, without the haze of propaganda and political correctness obscuring them. I base my belief on what I've seen during my travels to hundreds of campuses. Aside from the noisy protestors, some students come to hear my message with an open mind, understanding that they are in college to learn. At least the message is worth considering and discussing, they say. Others go further, motivated to question the given leftist wisdom. When students hear about free enterprise ideas and the Constitution, they end up liking the ideas. Still others enthusiastically join us at TP USA in our mission.

And so, I close on an optimistic note. A Reuters/Ipsos national opinion poll has discovered that among Millennials, the enthusiasm for the Democratic Party is waning. The online survey of more than sixteen thousand registered voters ages eighteen to thirty-four surveyed online shows their support for congressional Democrats over Republicans slipped significantly over the past two years.

When asked, "If the election for U.S. Congress were held today, would you vote for the Democratic candidate or the Republican candidate for U.S. Congress in your district where you live?" Forty-six percent said they would prefer the Democrat compared with 28 percent for the Republican. That's still a significant difference, but compared with 2016, 55 percent said they would vote for the Democrat and 27 percent for the Republican. That's a nine percentage-point drop in Democratic support. However, they don't appear to be transferring their loyalties to Republicans, which means that conservatives need to do a better job of explaining the benefits of liberty and the free market.

But here's the thing. Millennials are increasingly seeing Republicans as a better steward of the economy. According to Reuters, "Millennials are almost evenly split this year over the question of which party has a better plan for the economy, with 34 percent picking the Democrats and 32 percent choosing Republicans. That's a shift from two years ago, when they said Democrats had the better plan by a 12-point margin."

Ashley Reed, a white single mother of three in New Hampshire whom Reuters interviewed, might be typical. A teenage fascination with Barack Obama led her to support his presidency in 2008. "But her politics evolved with her personal life. Reed, now twenty-eight, grew more supportive of gun rights, for instance, while married to her now ex-husband, a U.S. Navy technician. She lost faith in social welfare programs she came to believe were misused. She opposed abortion after having children. Reed plans to vote for a Republican for Congress this year."

I love America and my passion is working with students who want to hear about liberty and freedom. This generation, my generation, is one that values freedom. It need not fall victim to leftist, dehumanizing evangelism. With the right organization, we can win back the future.

16

Join Us in Our Fight
for America's Soul

Turning Point USA has so successfully ignited a conservative movement on America's campuses that the left has taken to name-calling. A good measure of how successful you are is the desperate tone of the personal attacks launched against you.

And the assaults on Turning Point USA have become more and more frantic. We have been accused of being racist, homophobic, misogynist, and practically every other name in the leftist script. We have been charged with "openly promoting hatred and bigotry," accusations that are so unfounded that it's a waste of time bothering to counter them. Rare are the liberals who are willing to engage in a rational discussion over the merits and substance of our mission, which is to promote liberty and the free market.

It would be a perfect opportunity for us to resort to the same blather that the left always spouts: We are victims.

But instead of claiming victimhood, we wear the left-wing assaults as a badge of honor. Our successes have been many. When I founded Turning Point USA in 2012, I set out on a mission to build the most organized and powerful conservative grassroots activist network on America's college campuses. Now, Turning Point USA has become the largest and fastest growing youth organization in America.

Our rapidly expanded reach can be measured by my growing presence on campus and elsewhere. I have met with President Donald Trump more than fifteen times since his inauguration. I am the second most powerful tweeter in conservative politics, according to an independently ranked list. I've appeared on cable news shows more than five hundred times. And I've raised more than thirty million dollars for TPUSA in six years.

But it's not about me. All this exposure has allowed TPUSA to hire a full-time staff of 150 dedicated experts that identifies, educates, trains, and organizes students to promote the principles of freedom, free markets, and limited government. We have organized more than five thousand events, trained more than five thousand conservative Millennials, and conducted more than five hundred thousand face-to-face conversations—the most effective method of engagement. We have launched more than 350 TPUSA chapters and provided over 750 like-minded student groups with resources such as activism supplies, leadership training, and field staff support.

Our National Field Program provides representatives to help student leaders start a campus chapter, build membership, schedule programs, arrange popular speakers, and combat left-wing tactics of intolerance and bias against conservatives in higher education. For years, the left has dominated college campuses with paid field organizers, daily activism initiatives, and endless waves of leftist propaganda. But with a grassroots presence on more than one thousand college campuses nationwide, Turning Point USA has a stronger, more organized presence than all of the left-wing campus groups combined.

Now, we are armed with the largest national database of students who believe in capitalism and free markets. We are uniting young conservatives, from East Coast to West Coast, from public and private schools, to create a powerful national force to counter the liberal grip on higher education. We are motivating students to continue their activism in their communities after leaving the campus. All of these efforts are designed to achieve our ultimate goal: to educate students and the next generation of American leaders about the importance of free market values through well-planned, effective initiatives.

But wait, there's more. Our conferences attract thousands of committed and enthusiastic students to hear the most popular and most dynamic conservative speakers in America. Donald Trump Jr., Candace Owens, Dennis Prager, Dinesh D'Souza, Ben Shapiro, Brian Kilmeade, Scott Walker, Greg Gutfeld, and others wowed more than three thousand students at our 2017 Student Action Summit in West Palm Beach. Our slate of conferences is unparalleled: Young Women's Leadership Summit, Young Black Leadership Summit, Young Hispanic Leadership Summit, Chapter Leadership Summit, High School Leadership Summit, and regional leadership conferences. Fired-up attendees return to their campuses with a renewed commitment to liberty.

Our social media reach is exploding exponentially. I reach more than seven million people a day on my personal social media, and Turning Point USA reaches more than thirty-two million people a week. We constantly are working to re-brand free market values. With sound bites like "Big Government Sucks" and the incorporation of pop culture into our brand, we are able to reach new demographics and continuously expand the base.

Our Professor Watch List (https://www.professorwatchlist.org) has received national attention for exposing and documenting college professors who discriminate against conservative students and advance leftist propaganda in the classroom. It is an aggregated list of pre-existing news stories that were published by a variety of news organizations. Among those spotlighted is a professor who, in response to the pro-life March for Life, instructed its supporters to "sit down and shut up" because they are "racist." The list includes professors who sniff hatred and a long list of phobias in anyone who identifies as conservative.

Turning Point News (https://www.turningpoint.news) keeps young conservatives updated about the latest liberal outrages. Just one example: A student at a Jesuit university said he was leaving the school because of "rampant political bias" that is divorcing the school from the Catholic Church. He said students would shout "trigger warning" when walking past him in the hallway, with one even warning that he would be "hunted down" if he entered the school's intercultural center. Updated frequently, Turning Point News reveals the depth of the nastiness, dishonesty, and silliness that infects the campus left-wing establishment.

Our website (http://www.tpusa.com) provides a host of weapons for engaging the left. You can learn how to start a chapter on your campus. You can connect with chapters on other campuses. You can peruse the vast array of pamphlets and brochures featuring the conservative viewpoint on a variety of issues. Get posters to hang in your dorm room or to use when tabling to recruit new members. Or just come to know that you aren't alone.

Whether you just need to reinforce your beliefs or create a game plan to fight for your rights on your campus, join our community reach out to (https://www.tpusa.com/GetInvolved). If you have any questions or aren't sure where to start, feel free to email: info@tpusa.com.

We are gratified and honored by the response that we receive, whether from dedicated conservatives or just those who are curious about what they're not being taught at their schools. As I said in this book's introduction, I am encouraged by the response we receive on campuses across the nation and, more significantly, I'm truly convinced that a growing movement of young men and women are looking for a change. They are fed up with the tired preachments from the Book of the Left. They sense that the philosophy of soft expectations and victimhood that poisons young minds is a formula for failure. They reject the notion that socialism is America's natural and inevitable progression into a utopian dream world. They're weary of being told to shut up and listen. They're angered by ideologues who, in their arrogance, believe that silencing conservative expression conforms to America's highest ideals.

They are America's hope. They are America's answer to the autocratic, left-wing policies and politics that are robbing Americans of the potential that's their birthright. Thanks to them, liberty and free markets will flourish.

About the Author

Charlie Kirk is the Founder and Executive Director of Turning Point USA, a national student movement dedicated to identifying, organizing, and empowering young people to promote the principles of free markets and limited government.

Since the inception of Turning Point USA in June 2012, Charlie has grown Turning Point USA from nothing, to having representation on over 1,100 high schools and college campuses nationwide, with over seventy-five full time field staff.

At twenty-four years old, he has appeared on Fox News, CNBC, and FOX Business News over two hundred times, including frequent appearances on "Your World with Neil Cavuto," and "Varney & Co." Charlie is also the author of *Time for a Turning Point*.